House of Commons

Committee on the Lord Chancellor's Department

Children and Family Court Advisory and Support Service (CAFCASS)

Third Report of Session 2002-03

Volume I

Report, together with formal minutes

*Ordered by The House of Commons
to be printed 15 July 2003*

HC 614–I
Published on 23 July 2003
by authority of the House of Commons
London: The Stationery Office Limited
£13.00

The Committee on the Lord Chancellor's Department

The Committee on the Lord Chancellor's Department is appointed by the House of Commons to examine the expenditure, administration, and policy of the Lord Chancellor's Department and associated public bodies.

Current membership

Rt Hon Alan Beith MP (*Liberal Democrat, Berwick-upon-Tweed*) (Chairman)
Peter Bottomley MP (*Conservative, Worthing West*)
Mr James Clappison MP (*Conservative, Hertsmere*)
Ross Cranston MP (*Labour, Dudley North*)
Mrs Ann Cryer MP (*Labour, Keighley*)
Mr Jim Cunningham MP (*Labour, Coventry South*)
Mr Hilton Dawson MP (*Labour, Lancaster and Wyre*)
Mr Mark Field MP (*Conservative, Cities of London and Westminster*)
Mr Clive Soley MP (*Labour, Ealing, Acton and Shepherd's Bush*)
Keith Vaz MP (*Labour, Leicester East*)
Dr Alan Whitehead MP (*Labour, Southampton Test*)

Powers

The committee is one of the departmental select committees, the powers of which are set out in House of Commons Standing Orders, principally in SO No 152. These are available on the Internet via www.parliament.uk.

Publications

The Reports and evidence of the Committee are published by The Stationery Office by Order of the House. A list of Reports of the Committee in the present Session is at the back of this volume.

All publications of the Committee (including press notices) are on the Internet at www.parliament.uk/parliamentary_committees/lcd.cfm.

Committee staff

The current staff of the Committee are Huw Yardley (Clerk), Richard Poureshagh (Committee Assistant) and Julie Storey (Secretary).

Contacts

All correspondence should be addressed to the Clerk of the Committee on the Lord Chancellor's Department, House of Commons, 7 Millbank, London SW1P 3JA. The telephone number for general enquiries is 020 7219 8196. The Committee's email address is lcdcom@parliament.uk.

Contents

Report

		Page
	Summary	5
1	**Introduction**	7
	Our inquiry	7
	Acknowledging the devotion of CAFCASS practitioners	8
	Submissions from non-resident parents and those concerned about domestic violence	8
2	**The role of CAFCASS**	9
	Introduction to CAFCASS's role	9
	Private law proceedings	*9*
	Public law proceedings	*9*
	Other proceedings	*10*
	CAFCASS Legal Services and Special Casework	*10*
	Wider responsibilities	*10*
	Role of MCSI	11
3	**The establishment of CAFCASS**	12
	Aim of the new service	12
	Problems with the establishment of the service	13
	Timetable	*13*
	Work of the Project Team	14
	Effect of the short timetable	*15*
	Appointment of the Board and senior management team	15
	Funding	*17*
	Establishment of the service: conclusion	*17*
4	**The early days**	19
	Dispute with self-employed guardians	19
	Disruption in the senior management team	*21*
	Role of the Lord Chancellor's Department	22
	Intervention by LCD officials	*22*
	Suspicions of cost-cutting	*23*
	Tandem representation	*23*
	Work of the Project Team	24
	Review by the National Audit Office	25
5	**Current situation**	26
	Failures in service provision	26
	Reasons for delay	*27*
	CAFCASS Legal	*28*
	Lowering of standards for recruitment	*28*
	Training	29

	Consequences of the lack of training	*30*
	Convergence	*30*
	Performance management and appraisal	*31*
	Information Technology	32
	Support services	33
	Partnership funding	*33*
	Effect of LCD's PSA targets	*34*
	Relations with the Legal Services Commission	*34*
	Relations with other organisations	35
	Research and improving practice	36
6	**Corporate governance**	**38**
	Management and organisational culture	38
	Management	*38*
	Internal communications and relations with front-line staff	*39*
	The "mixed economy"	*40*
	Relationship between LCD and CAFCASS	42
	The CAFCASS Board	45
7	**The way forward**	**47**
	Failures in service provision	47
	CAFCASS Legal	*49*
	Dealing with the backlog	*49*
	Recruitment and workforce planning	49
	Attracting back experienced guardians	*51*
	Longer-term recruitment	*51*
	Standard of work done by new recruits	*51*
	Training and professional development	51
	Induction training	*52*
	Convergence	*52*
	Performance management	*53*
	Progress in the provision of training	*53*
	Information Technology	54
	Support services	55
	Need to indicate role in provision of support services	*55*
	Funding for support services	*56*
	Cooperation with other bodies	*57*
	Research and improving practice	58
	Management and organisational culture	58
	The Framework Document and CAFCASS's relationship with government	60
	The CAFCASS Board	60
	Inspection regime	*62*
	Continued Parliamentary scrutiny of CAFCASS's work	*62*
	Conclusions and recommendations	**63**

Witnesses	**71**
List of written evidence	**72**
Reports from the Committee on the Lord Chancellor's Department	**76**

Summary

The Children and Family Court Advisory and Support Service (CAFCASS) was established on 1 April 2001. It brought together the work of securing children's welfare through representation and reporting previously done by the Family Court Welfare Service, the Guardian ad Litem and Reporting Officer panels and the Children's Division of the Official Solicitor. At the time our inquiry started, CAFCASS fell within the responsibility of the Lord Chancellor; that responsibility has now been transferred to the Minister for Children in the Department for Education and Skills.

The skill and devotion of staff throughout the organisation and their commitment to the children they serve is not to be gainsaid, and criticisms of the way CAFCASS's difficulties have been handled should not detract from that. Nevertheless, widespread concern about CAFCASS's performance has been apparent ever since it was set up. A dispute with the self-employed guardians who made up the bulk of the pre-CAFCASS workforce on the public law side of the new organisation's work led to a loss of staff which had a serious impact on CAFCASS's ability to deliver core services. CAFCASS found itself unable to cope with increasing demand for its services and significant delays in the allocation of guardians to cases persisted. Meanwhile CAFCASS failed to improve the service offered by the Family Court Welfare Service in private law disputes. Many vulnerable children were left without full representation at critical times as a result.

Our inquiry found serious failings in the establishment and management of the new Service. Too little time was allowed for its establishment, leaving the organisation at a disadvantage from the start. Once established, CAFCASS failed to make proper use of the preparatory work which had been done, compounding the difficulties. Relations with self-employed guardians were mishandled, resulting in the alienation of an important sector of the workforce. The focus on the dispute and an over-emphasis on the creation of management structures led to the neglect of other important aspects of the service, including training and professional development, IT and the development of support services for children and families experiencing relationship breakdown. Meanwhile, the delivery of CAFCASS's core services failed to improve.

A CAFCASS Board lacking experience and expertise in key areas of the organisation's work proved unable to exercise effective oversight or provide appropriate strategic direction, hindered by confusion over lines of accountability and the respective roles of the Board, the senior management team and the Lord Chancellor's Department. The dismissal of the original Chief Executive caused further disruption to CAFCASS's work, while LCD itself managed to create the impression that its prime interest in the new Service was in keeping costs down.

We make a number of recommendations aimed at enabling CAFCASS to become the "high quality service operating to the best professional standards" envisaged when it was first proposed. The priority for CAFCASS must be for it to get to grips with its service delivery duties, and clear the backlog of cases which has been allowed to build up. To assist in doing so, it should conduct a comprehensive workforce planning exercise aimed at ensuring that it knows what resources are needed. It should establish a dedicated training and professional development strand and enable the effective performance management of its front-line practitioners. It should put in place a fully fledged case management system which will allow the collation of reliable information for management and research purposes and relieve some of the burden on hard-pressed front-line managers. It should indicate the role it envisages for itself in the provision of support services, and develop relations with other bodies working in the field, particularly the Legal Services Commission. Additionally, it should develop its research capacity so that it can establish "what works" for children experiencing family breakdown.

Changes are also required in corporate governance. CAFCASS needs to demonstrate clearly and unambiguously that it is putting children and young people first in all it does. It should re-examine its management structures with a view to ensuring that it has a management style appropriate to the work it does. CAFCASS's Framework Document should be rewritten so that it explicitly reflects the Service's core tasks and sets out the proper constitutional relationship between CAFCASS as an NDPB and its parent Department. There should be a fundamental review of membership of the Board, with the aim of bringing onto it people of experience and stature who can develop the strategy necessary to deliver an effective, child-centred service. The new Board should take steps to ensure that it is able to carry out effectively its function of providing strategic direction and holding senior management to account.

CAFCASS performs a vitally important function in the protection of vulnerable children at a critical time in their lives. In the two years of its existence so far considerable doubt has been cast on its ability to perform that function effectively. CAFCASS needs to be helped to use, develop and build on the considerable skills which exist among its personnel and to become the kind of quality organisation it was originally intended to be. We hope that by addressing the concerns raised in this Report CAFCASS will begin to regain the confidence of those working with and for it and show that it is an organisation genuinely and effectively committed to the children it serves.

1 Introduction

1. The Children and Family Court Advisory and Support Service, generally known by its acronym, CAFCASS, was formally established on 1 April 2001. It is a non-departmental public body accountable, at the time our inquiry started, to the Lord Chancellor. Following the machinery of government changes announced by the Prime Minister on 13 June,[1] responsibility for CAFCASS will now transfer to the Department for Education and Skills, under the Minister for Children. The organisation's role is to provide a service to the Courts in family proceedings. In the words of CAFCASS itself, "CAFCASS exists to ensure children and young people are put first in family proceedings; that their voices are properly heard; that the decisions made about them by courts are in their best interests; and that they and their families are supported throughout the process."[2]

Our inquiry

2. Our decision to inquire into the work of CAFCASS followed widespread concern about the organisation's performance. That concern has been apparent ever since the inception of the service in April 2001. Negotiations preceding the establishment of the new service led to a dispute with the self-employed guardians who, at that time, undertook the vast majority of the work on the public law side in most parts of the country.[3] As a result, many left the service, and the consequent lack of staff resulted in increasing delays in the allocation of guardians to cases in public law.[4] The problems were compounded by allegations of mismanagement at senior levels within CAFCASS which culminated in the suspension and eventual dismissal of the Chief Executive.[5] Despite the assurance of the Lord Chancellor, in evidence to the Home Affairs Committee in October 2001, that he was "very much on the case",[6] the impression continued to grow of a service in crisis. The importance of the work which CAFCASS undertakes—safeguarding the proper protection of some of the most vulnerable children in our society—led us to announce shortly after our own establishment an inquiry into the work of the organisation.

3. The importance of the work of CAFCASS, and the widespread nature of the concern over its performance, were reflected in the large number of submissions which we received. Nearly 80 individuals and organisations sent us written memoranda. We heard oral evidence from 12 of these, in addition to CAFCASS itself and the responsible Minister. A number of us also undertook visits to CAFCASS offices in our local areas.

4. We are grateful to all of those who submitted evidence, both written and oral, and to those who arranged and participated in the visits we undertook to local offices. We also express our thanks to our specialist advisers, Professor Judith Masson of the University of

---

[1] Number 10 press notice 13/06/2003, *Reform of children's services: Margaret Hodge appointed Minister of State for Children*

[2] CAFCASS Corporate Plan 2003/06, p 7

[3] See paras 36–42 below

[4] See paras 60–67 below

[5] See paras 43–46 below

[6] Home Affairs Committee, *Minutes of Evidence: The Rt Hon Lord Irvine of Lairg QC, and Sir Hayden Phillips KCB, The Work of the Lord Chancellor's Department*, HC (2001–02) 269, Q 114

Warwick and Professor Adrian James of the University of Bradford, for their help and guidance throughout this inquiry.

Acknowledging the devotion of CAFCASS practitioners

5. Before we set out our findings in relation to the work of CAFCASS, **we wish to acknowledge the skill and devotion of staff throughout the organisation and their commitment to the children they serve.** CAFCASS officer is a vital profession, and those who choose to take it up deserve every encouragement as well as recognition for the work they do. Throughout its difficult early period, CAFCASS has continued to be staffed by people who have worked very hard to achieve the best outcomes they could for the children for whom they are responsible. **The criticisms we make of the way CAFCASS's difficulties have been handled should not detract from that fact.**

Submissions from non-resident parents and those concerned about domestic violence

6. We also wish to respond to the submissions we have received relating to CAFCASS officers' practice in cases involving disputes over children's contact with non-resident parents, and where domestic violence has been an issue. The concerns which have been raised by these groups and individuals are many and varied. These issues have not been the focus of our inquiry, and we have not carried out any detailed investigations in connection with them. The most that we can say is that much more research needs to be done in this area, and we make recommendations below about how CAFCASS should address this need.[7] Without such research, we cannot comment on the quality of work done in individual cases.

---

[7] Para 166

2 The role of CAFCASS

Introduction to CAFCASS's role

7. Proceedings in which CAFCASS officers are involved may broadly be divided into two categories: private law proceedings, predominantly where parties (usually, but not exclusively, parents) cannot reach agreement on the best arrangements for the child; and public law proceedings, which concern applications for local authority care or supervision and other care related matters. CAFCASS officers are appointed by the Court to provide a report and, depending on the nature of the proceedings, to fulfil the respective functions of Children and Family Reporter, Children's Guardian, Reporting Officer or Parental Reporter.

8. The Criminal Justice and Court Services Act 2000 provides that the primary duties of CAFCASS in respect of family proceedings are to:

a) Safeguard and promote the welfare of the children

b) Give advice to any Court about any application made to it in such proceedings

c) Make provision for the children to be represented in such proceedings, and

d) Provide information, advice and other support for the children and their families.[8]

Private law proceedings

9. The principal role of the Children and Family Reporter is to investigate and report on issues concerning the welfare of children involved in disputes about residence and contact, at the request of the court. The role has traditionally been described as "acting as the eyes and ears of the Court." The Children and Family Reporter may also assist parents to resolve any outstanding areas of disagreement, if this is possible during the course of their enquiries. CAFCASS is also responsible for the supervision of family assistance orders when these are made.[9]

Public law proceedings

10. The role of the children's guardian (formerly "guardian ad litem") in public law proceedings is set out in the Children Act 1989 and accompanying court rules.[10] The child is a party to these proceedings; the children's guardian represents the child, appointing and instructing the solicitor for the child in most cases, investigating fully the child's circumstances, advising the court about the management of the proceedings and preparing

---

[8] Criminal Justice and Court Services Act 2000, s 12(1)

[9] Children Act 1989 s 16 gave courts the power to make a family assistance order in exceptional circumstances and, with the agreement of those adults named in the order, to assist families with any continuing problems post-divorce. The assistance offered is defined as voluntary.

[10] Children Act 1989, ss 41 and 42; Family Proceedings Rules 1991, rr 10, 11 and 11A

a report advising the court on the child's interests. In order to complete this work the guardian normally has direct contact with the child in order to establish their wishes and feelings, reads social services files concerning the child, interviews members of the child's family and makes a professional assessment of the child's welfare, sometimes with the assistance of reports from experts.

Other proceedings

11. CAFCASS officers also act in two other types of proceedings. In proceedings under the Adoption Act 1976 (soon to be replaced by the Adoption and Children Act 2002), a CAFCASS officer will act either as a Reporting Officer or as a Children's Guardian, depending on the circumstances. CAFCASS also acts as Parental Reporter in applications under the Human Fertilisation and Embryology Act 1990.

CAFCASS Legal Services and Special Casework

12. CAFCASS Legal has taken over the role previously played by the Official Solicitor (Children's Division) in providing confidential advice to civil courts and representing children where there are issues of legal or moral complexity central to their welfare. In such circumstances CAFCASS Legal will act as the child's solicitor. Examples of circumstances where CAFCASS Legal might become involved include cases where there are disputes over major medical treatment, including life or death decisions, or proceedings which raise new challenges to practice under the Human Rights Act 1998. CAFCASS Legal can also become involved in complex disputes over residence and contact in private law cases where there are concerns about the welfare of the child.

Wider responsibilities

13. CAFCASS has also been entrusted by Parliament with additional responsibilities beyond the core service of advising the courts in family proceedings. The new unified service was originally proposed as simply the Children and Family Court Advisory Service.[11] By the time the Bill which was to set up the service was presented to Parliament, an additional 'S', for Support, had been added to its title. This change of title was reflected in section 12(1)(d) of the Act, which gave CAFCASS the duty to "provide information, advice and other support for the children and their families." CAFCASS declares itself to have a role as a "children's champion", making an active input to broader policy development across Government and bringing its knowledge and independent perspective to the development of policies to improve services for children.[12]

---

[11] *Single Service to Safeguard Interests of Children in Family Courts*, Lord Chancellor's Department Press Notice, 27 July 1999

[12] CAFCASS Corporate Plan 2003/06, p 8

Role of MCSI

14. CAFCASS is subject to inspection by the CAFCASS Inspection Unit of HM Magistrates' Court Services Inspectorate (MCSI). MCSI has produced a number of reports on CAFCASS since launch, including two "overview" reports: *Setting Up*, published in March 2002; and *Setting a Course*, published in April this year.[13]

---

[13] Available from www.mcsi.gov.uk

3 The establishment of CAFCASS

Aim of the new service

15. The formation of a unified service was proposed in a Government consultation paper published in July 1998.[14] The new service would subsume the work previously done by:

- the Probation Service through Family Court Welfare;

- the Guardian ad Litem and Reporting Officer (GALRO) Service, organised through local panels, mostly administered by local authorities; and

- the Children's Division of the Official Solicitor.

The high regard in which each of these predecessor services was held was emphasised, and the aims of the new organisation were intended to mirror those of the existing services. The intention was that the integration of these services into one organisation should bring longer-term advantages, including greater flexibility in the deployment of resources and opportunities to enhance the overall service through any resulting savings.[15]

16. However, there were other concerns which lay behind the establishment of a new service. One of these was the position of the family court welfare (FCW) service within the Probation Service. Expenditure on FCW work accounted for less than 10% of Probation Service spending and staff resources.[16] We were told that it had been marginalised by its host organisation, the Probation Service, for many years, and that there was some evidence that the service was not always able to carry out its core task effectively because of managerial pressure on throughput.[17] The administration of the GALRO service through local authorities[18] was also considered less than entirely satisfactory. There were wide variations in practice across the country, as had been indicated in the overviews of annual GALRO reports undertaken by the Social Services Inspectorate, and in research.[19] Importantly, there was also limited scope for Panel Managers to exercise effective control over quality and cost-effectiveness. It was hoped that CAFCASS would be in a better position to address these issues and to develop mechanisms for ensuring cost-effectiveness while maintaining, and where necessary, raising, the level of service.[20]

17. Nevertheless, the establishment of the new service was very far from being simply a reaction to perceived deficiencies in existing services. It was hoped that the bringing together of the family court work done in public and private law would enable cross-

---

[14] *Support Services in Family Proceedings – Future Organisation of Court Welfare Services*, Department of Health, Home Office, Lord Chancellor's Department and Welsh Office, July 1998

[15] *ibid*, para 1.31

[16] *ibid*, para 1.13

[17] Ev 126 para 22

[18] Local authorities were permitted to contract out their responsibilities for day-to-day administration of the GALRO service to a voluntary organisation or other body; at the time of publication of the consultation paper, 5 GALRO panels were contracted out in this way, all to voluntary child care organisations (*Support Services in Family Proceedings, op cit*, para 1.22)

[19] Ev 124 paras 9–12

[20] Ev 24 para 3, 247 para 4(vii)

fertilisation between the roles of children's guardian and family court welfare officer, and facilitate the spreading of best practice. The new service would also be ideally placed to develop a much-needed support and advice role for children and families experiencing breakdown. Finally, it was hoped that, with the greater freedom of a non-departmental public body, CAFCASS could bring an independent perspective to bear on the development of family law and policy, acting as a "children's champion" in this area of government.

18. The new service was not, therefore, intended to be merely "business as usual", even within its core services.[21] The 1998 consultation paper set out the aim of

> a high quality service operating to the best professional standards. It will build on the high quality of existing services. It will be staffed mainly by professionals with a social work or legal background. It will be effectively managed and administered within clear legal obligations and nationally agreed standards of performance. It will demonstrate efficient use of all its resources. Its focus is on the welfare of children before the courts at a time when crucial decisions about their future are being taken. At the same time, it will be a service which, through its other responsibilities, makes a wider contribution to the welfare of families likely to be involved in family proceedings…[22]

As the responsible Minister said during debate on the Bill which was to establish CAFCASS, "It will not simply replicate existing services. … Our intention is that it should build on the strengths of the existing three services in order to provide a better, more child-focused and flexible service."[23]

Problems with the establishment of the service

19. The circumstances in which CAFCASS was brought into being, however, made early fulfilment of the hopes for the new service an almost impossible task. CAFCASS's setup was hindered by three key difficulties:

- the truncated timetable for establishment

- the delayed appointment of the Board and senior management team, and

- inadequate initial funding.

Timetable

20. The July 1998 consultation paper said that it was unlikely that a unified service could be established in less than three years, and that it could take up to five.[24] In July 1999, the Government announced its intention to establish a new National Probation Service, under the Home Office's responsibility, and, at the same time, CAFCASS under the Lord

---

[21] Ev 202 para 3
[22] *op cit*, para 3.3
[23] Stg Co Deb, Standing Committee G, *Criminal Justice and Court Services Bill*, Tuesday 11 April 2000
[24] *op cit*, para 6.1

Chancellor.[25] In March 2000, the Criminal Justice and Court Services Bill, providing for the establishment of both new services, was published. The Bill received Royal Assent on 30 November 2000.[26] CAFCASS itself was launched on 1 April 2001. This was less than three years after the publication of the consultation paper, and less than two years after the announcement of the final decision to create the new service.

21. The decision to launch CAFCASS on 1 April 2001 was principally determined by the Home Office's timetable for establishment of the new National Probation Service on the same date.[27] The establishment of CAFCASS could not, the Department argued, have been delayed without causing unacceptable disruption to the Family Court Welfare Service.[28]

22. The Department's memorandum goes on to summarise the resulting difficulties:

> The period between CAFCASS's founding legislation being in place (delayed by a longer than expected Parliamentary process) and launch of the new Service in April 2001 proved, with hindsight, to be too short a timespan for all the changes that were needed. In particular, it did not allow a period of shadow running for the Board and senior managers. This would have provided an opportunity for those who would oversee the new Service to become familiar with their new responsibilities and with the operating structures that would make up CAFCASS; allowing greater planning by those who would run the Service of the new processes and policies it would need. It was always planned that the new Service would be launched with a mandate to evolve, on the basis of operating experience, to best deliver its functions. Nevertheless, the truncated timetable and the view of the Inland Revenue, in the run up to CAFCASS's launch, that the self-employed guardians' contracts were unlikely to deliver self-employed tax status significantly increased the challenges the new organisation faced on launch.[29]

Work of the Project Team

23. The establishment of the Service was preceded by preparatory work undertaken by an inter-departmental Project Team in the Lord Chancellor's Department, with officials from the Home Office, the Department of Health and the Welsh Office. The Team's Project Director took up post in October 1999. The Team oversaw the CAFCASS provisions of the Bill through their Parliamentary progress. In parallel, they planned for the new Service. They undertook all the detailed arrangements for implementation, including transfer of all parts of the services which would become CAFCASS into the new organisation from April 2001.[30]

24. The Department told us that preparation for the new Service "relied on widespread involvement of staff and stakeholders who would work with CAFCASS and its services." The Project Team set up Advisory Groups and Task Teams to input views as the Service

---

[25] "Single service to safeguard interests of children in family courts", LCD press notice 199–99, 27 July 1999
[26] Ev 203 para 6
[27] *ibid*, para 7
[28] *ibid*
[29] *ibid*, para 8
[30] *ibid*, para 9

was developed. Stakeholder groups were set up to advise as development of CAFCASS's IT, staffing and estate transfer were taken forward. These groups were, the Department says, "instrumental in shaping the structure of the Service." Stakeholders were also involved through a number of advisory groups, which included representatives of, among others, the judiciary, family law practitioners, and mothers' and fathers' representative groups. The Project Team appeared at major conferences to publicise and answer questions about CAFCASS. They attended over 100 local meetings with members of the Family Court Welfare Service, the guardians' profession, the judiciary and legal profession. Several conferences across England and Wales were arranged by the Project Team for staff considering transferring into the new Service.[31]

25. According to the Department, "Views put forward were fed into the Project Team's work as far as possible, but there were inevitably ideas that stretched beyond set up. Some were aspirational and would take time to develop or deliver." "It was envisaged," the Department continues, "[that] the Service would take forward this development work once established."[32]

Effect of the short timetable

26. As the Department admits, the short timetable on which CAFCASS was set up proved to be a significant handicap to its successful establishment as an organisation. This is of course easy to say with the benefit of hindsight; more difficult when the desire for change and development is prevalent and other factors seem to militate in favour of minimal delay.[33] **Nonetheless the decision to proceed on that timetable was a serious misjudgement.** Furthermore, it is difficult to argue that the problems only became apparent once the organisation had been established, when the consultation paper proposing its establishment recognised that three to five years would be needed to put it on a proper footing. **The Government should not have allowed the timetable for the establishment of the National Probation Service to dictate the unrealistic programme for the establishment of CAFCASS. The decision to do so makes CAFCASS appear of secondary importance. The impression was gained that the Departmental priorities of the Lord Chancellor's Department were secondary to those of the Home Office. It is vital that all Government Ministers give priority to work with children in line with their commitments under the UN Convention on the Rights of the Child.**

Appointment of the Board and senior management team

27. The truncated timetable made it all the more important that a shadow Board and senior management team be put in place in good time for 'vesting day' on 1 April 2001. That did not happen. The closing date for applications for the Chair and members of the Board was 30 June 2000. Interviews for Board members were held in September; the chair was appointed in December 2000; but the other successful candidates were not informed of

---

[31] *ibid*, para 12

[32] *ibid*

[33] See MCSI report, *Setting Up*, para 1.3, which reports opinion "sharply divided" on whether more preparatory time should have been allowed, but also suggests that opinion swung further towards the view that it should as the difficulties became more apparent

their appointment until a letter of 10 January 2001. The first Board meeting did not take place until 13 February 2001.[34]

28. The Department had also failed to assemble a full senior management team, and a number of posts were filled on an interim basis or by consultants.[35] A memorandum to this inquiry from the then Director of Operations describes the situation at that time:

> It is worth noting that the establishment of the new National Probation Service, although hugely complex in itself, was assisted and enabled by a more fully developed 'shadow' appointed HQ Directorate staff pending the passage of the relevant legislation, whereas the development of CAFCASS appears to have been left largely to poorly managed consultants. For example, on taking up my post my daily consultancy bill was approximately £4,500: information and IT (c. £2,000); estates (c. £1,200); my predecessor, retained by the CE (c. £800); communication (c. £500). It was clear that these consultants (broadly speaking) were doing their best, but in a management vacuum.[36]

Quite apart from the operational difficulties which this situation would have caused, the daily expenditure of these sums on consultants appears to us to be a questionable use of scarce resources.

29. The advantages the presence of a full Board and senior management team would have brought to the planning of the new service are noted by the Department itself in the quotation above.[37] A properly functioning shadow Board could have alerted Ministers to the serious problems being experienced in preparing for the establishment of the Service, or done more to ensure a "firm hand on the tiller" during that difficult period. Even if a shadow Board had not been able to influence the timetable for the establishment of CAFCASS, its timely formation would at least have enabled its members to gain experience and understanding of the work of the new organisation and the challenges facing it before it formally started work.[38] The importance of having a full senior management team in place from the start when dealing with all the complications of bringing together policies, practitioners and administrative and management staff from so many different predecessor organisations should have been self-evident. The Department asserts that delay to Royal Assent of CAFCASS's founding legislation truncated the recruitment timetable for senior posts and for planning for the transfer of staff and contractors into the new Service.[39] **Contingency plans should, however, have been in place to deal with such an eventuality. In particular, it is difficult to understand why a shadow Board was not set up, with an indication that permanent appointment was subject to the passage of the Bill.[40]**

---

[34] Ev 227
[35] Ev 107 para 4.3, 216
[36] Ev 216
[37] Para 22
[38] *ibid*
[39] Ev 205 para 25
[40] Ev 250–251 (Q 199) para 1, 226 para 1.1

Funding

30. CAFCASS's original budget also turned out to be inadequate. The year one running cost budget was just under £72m, to which 'start up' capital money of some £9m was added, making a total cash budget of just over £80.8m. The Department records that "significant work" was done by the Project Team to ensure the costing assumptions which produced these figures were soundly-based;[41] but continues,

> It was always going to be difficult ... to take full account of the total costs including the hidden overheads of support to the many small, locally-delivered services that made up CAFCASS. This was in part because such information was not routinely needed until CAFCASS was in prospect and then not easily obtainable or estimated across numerous localised operations.[42]

31. Subsequent budget increases (CAFCASS's budget for 2003–04 is £95m[43]) reveal the inadequacy of the original allocation. Despite the Department's assertion that the Project Team undertook "detailed scrutiny" of statistical returns for the Guardian service and annual reports from a number of probation service areas,[44] witnesses suggested to us that there was a failure properly to assess the actual, rather than the budgeted, costs of the service.[45] It has also been pointed out that there was an incentive for local authorities and the Probation Service to underestimate their actual spend on services which were to be transferred to CAFCASS, to minimise the cuts to their own funding.[46] That such factors should not have been taken into account when calculating the initial budget allocation suggests failure on the part of the Department to achieve sufficient resources to ensure that the Service could properly fulfil its remit.[47] Thus the deeply damaging impression was formed at an early stage that cost-cutting was part of the agenda leading to the establishment of the service: an impression which has persisted despite the later injections of cash from the Department.

Establishment of the service: conclusion

32. We deal in later paragraphs with the mistakes and failures which occurred after vesting day. However, **the overall impression gained from consideration of the circumstances leading up to the establishment of CAFCASS is that even prior to its establishment there was a lack of high-level effectiveness to ensure that the new service was a success.** The Minister has acknowledged that there were lessons to be learnt for the Department from the establishment of CAFCASS.[48] Nevertheless, **the mistakes and misjudgements made at that time left a legacy which made the already difficult task of creating a**

---

[41] Ev 204 para 14
[42] *ibid*, para 15
[43] CAFCASS Corporate Plan 2003–06, p 22
[44] Ev 204 para 14
[45] Ev 190 para 1.2, 251 s 2, 216; Q 217
[46] Ev 251 para 2.4
[47] See MCSI conclusion "There are significant expectations that CAFCASS as a new organisation covering England and Wales will provide a wider range of services to improved levels of quality. Where such expectations require additional funding, recognition is needed that this can only come via the usual route of interdepartmental bidding." (*Setting Up*, p 9)
[48] Q 301

successful new organisation even more difficult, and contributed significantly to some of the problems which are still being experienced.[49]

---

[49] Ev 124 para 5

4 The early days

33. Circumstances leading up to vesting day on 1 April 2001 were inauspicious. Matters were made worse by the events which took place in the early months of CAFCASS's formal existence. As CAFCASS itself and those representing the organisation have been at pains to point out, creating a new organisation from some 117 previous employing authorities was always going to be a difficult task. CAFCASS told us that "the scale of the challenge was underestimated",[50] and in view of the comments we make in the previous section it is impossible to disagree with that conclusion. But those presented with the task of meeting that challenge did not make it any easier by the way they approached it.

34. In particular, the early days were characterized by confusion in the governance arrangements for the new Service. In its Report on CAFCASS's first few months, published in March 2002, MCSI reported:

> Setting a culture and style for governance of any organisation is important. This process can be distorted if, through necessity or for other reasons, key people are temporarily acting out of role and there is, in consequence, a lack of clarity about respective responsibilities. There was evidence of some confusion around the respective functions of key organisational elements, including:
>
> — the Board, its Chairman and its Sub-Committees or Working Groups
>
> — the Chief Executive and the Senior Management Team
>
> — the interfaces between CAFCASS as a Non Departmental Public Body and its sponsoring organisation, the LCD.[51]

That confusion manifested itself in a number of different ways, and made a major contribution to some of CAFCASS's early difficulties.

Dispute with self-employed guardians

35. Almost immediately after its establishment CAFCASS became embroiled in a dispute with its self-employed guardians about the nature of the contracts they would be offered in the new service.

36. The history is as follows. Before CAFCASS's formal establishment, the inherited arrangements had been challenged by the Inland Revenue on the grounds that the existing contracts did not represent self-employment. Guardians had been offered, as an alternative to employment within the organisation, a self-employed contract based on a fixed fee scheme according to the length of time which a case was likely to take. This had, however, been rejected by NAGALRO, the organisation representing self-employed guardians, on a number of grounds. Guardians' particular concern was that the predetermination of the

---

[50] Ev 106 para 4.3
[51] *Setting Up*, para 2.4, page 29

amount of time allowed to work on a case would threaten their professional independence as officers of the Court.

37. Following the formal establishment of CAFCASS on 1 April 2001, and further negotiations aimed at producing a contract acceptable to self-employed guardians having failed, NAGALRO applied for judicial review of the decision to offer fixed-fee contracts. In response, CAFCASS took a decision at the end of June 2001 not to offer any self-employed contracts at all, and instead to operate a fully employed service. NAGALRO responded in turn by applying for judicial review of this decision. The judicial review was heard in September 2001. The decision to operate a fully managed service was quashed on the basis that it represented "a complete *volte-face*" on the part of CAFCASS, which had previously indicated that it would continue to offer self-employment and had offered no opportunity for those affected to make representations about why it should not now do so.[52]

38. Behind the history lies an unfortunate tale of conflict between self-employed guardians and CAFCASS senior management, the legacy of which is continuing to affect the Service today. Self-employed guardians have felt from the beginning that they were undervalued, and that their role was misunderstood by those planning the new service. Typical comments from the evidence we received included:

> The Guardians were harshly treated, and had to resort to judicial review to secure a barely equitable settlement…[53]

> It is now self-evident that trust has broken down between Guardians and CAFCASS. Whereas most Guardians had a strong investment in the reputation of their old panels, CAFCASS is now perceived as the enemy of a quality service to children…[54]

> I have watched with dismay the steady erosion of the role of Children's Guardian as welfare advocate for some of the most vulnerable children in our society…[55]

> Experienced practitioners do not feel that their skills are valued by the new organisation and this is especially true of self employed practitioners…[56]

> The long running dispute with self-employed guardians has discouraged and alienated experienced professionals in this field…[57]

39. For those self-employed guardians, the decision to offer a fixed-fee contract crystallised all their feelings about the Service and the way it was treating them. The fixed-fee contract appeared to guardians to betray a severe lack of understanding of the work they actually did. Historically, guardians had worked for an hourly rate, with a significant level of autonomy over the way they worked on a case. The change to a fixed-fee basis would, they argued, constrain to an unacceptable degree the way they were able to work on a case, and

---

[52] R (NALGALRO) v CAFCASS [2001] EWHC Admin 693; [2002] 1 FLR 255
[53] Ev 103
[54] Ev 117
[55] Ev 128
[56] Ev 135
[57] Ev 151

threaten their professional independence. The change did not take account of the impossibility of ascertaining, on allocation at the very beginning of a case, how complex the issues involved were likely to be, how long it would take, and ultimately how much work was likely to have to be done. The primary intention behind the original contract, in the view of the guardians, was to control costs.

40. The subsequent decision not to offer self-employed contracts at all was, if anything, even worse. This decision seemed to indicate that, if CAFCASS could not control self-employed guardians' work, and thus costs, through fixed-fee contracts, it simply did not want self-employed guardians at all. The overall impression guardians were left with was that they were not valued; if CAFCASS could not have them on its own terms, it did not want them at all.

41. Meanwhile, the necessity of dealing with the dispute with the self-employed guardians led to the neglect of certain other key aspects of the Service. There was little or no development of the policies and procedures which, as a new organisation, CAFCASS lacked; important issues of harmonisation of terms and conditions of staff inherited from the large number of previous employers were not addressed;[58] and other fundamental issues such as training and professional development, research, and IT were neglected.[59]

Disruption in the senior management team

42. We have already discussed the failure to establish the Board and senior management team in good time for the establishment of CAFCASS. It was in these early days after CAFCASS's formal establishment that the effects of that failure first began to be felt.

43. By the time of MCSI's first visit to CAFCASS Headquarters, in June 2001, the Chief Executive and a senior management team (SMT) were in place, although some senior management postholders were not permanent appointments. MCSI reported that at that time "a sense of SMT leadership was emerging as key posts were filled with permanent staff", and "considerable strategic thinking had been accomplished around finance, IT, communication and other operational issues."[60]

44. Despite that early encouragement, however, the senior management team did not, ultimately, work effectively. Tension between certain members of the team culminated in the departure of the Director of Operations in August 2001.[61] Subsequently, dissatisfaction with the performance of the Chief Executive herself grew, and led in November 2001 to her suspension. By the time of MCSI's second visit, in December 2001,

> inspectors were concerned that there was little common understanding of, or agreement about, the main planning processes whereby key policies were formulated and agreed within CAFCASS. Indeed, in some instances, there was fundamental disagreement as to whether certain policies had ever been discussed and agreed.[62]

---

[58] Ev 215
[59] Ev 215–216
[60] *Setting Up*, para 2.5
[61] Ev 215
[62] *Setting Up*, para 2.5

45. The details of the departure of the Director of Operations are not known, since he was required to sign a confidentiality agreement on departure. The suspension of the Chief Executive was followed, in July 2002, by her dismissal after a disciplinary inquiry. Subsequently, she took CAFCASS to an employment tribunal, which during the course of our inquiry was settled before a hearing took place.

46. Meanwhile, the Board was not functioning effectively either. The Board of an NDPB should not get involved in the day-to-day running of the organisation. It should, however, be able to exercise effective oversight of the strategic direction of the organisation, identify areas where problems are occurring, and ensure that action is taken to put them right. The CAFCASS Board was unable to perform this key role.

47. There is plenty of evidence for the Board's ineffectiveness. We have already noted MCSI's concerns about the way the Board was functioning.[63] One Board member has reported directly to us how her concerns, and those of other Board members, were ignored, and how the Board was expected to act merely as a rubber stamp for the proposals of the Chief Executive.[64] The Board's standing orders require it to meet in public at least twice a year: so far it has failed to hold even one meeting in public.[65] Published minutes of Board meetings are sketchy and give very little indication of how matters are progressed.[66] Most obvious, however, is the deterioration in service over which the Board has presided. No effective overseeing organisation could have allowed such a serious breakdown in the performance of the key functions for which it is responsible.

Role of the Lord Chancellor's Department

48. We discuss concerns about the relationship between CAFCASS and the Lord Chancellor's Department more fully later in this Report.[67] Much of what we say there about the performance of the Board throughout CAFCASS's existence is relevant to the early days. The lack of focus caused by the failure of the Framework Document properly to reflect CAFCASS's *raison d'être*, for example, was an important contributory factor in these initial difficulties. Here, however, we concentrate on two points: inappropriate early intervention in CAFCASS's operations by LCD officials; and suspicions that LCD approached the creation of CAFCASS with a covert cost-cutting agenda.

Intervention by LCD officials

49. A certain degree of interest on the part of Ministers in the operation of the new service was to be expected. It is reasonable to expect Ministers to pay close attention to the performance of such a vital organisation, and to ensure that their officials do so on their behalf. However, the establishment of CAFCASS as an NDPB implied a "hands-off" approach which the Department appears not fully to have respected. One example of this came in the handling of the dispute with the self-employed guardians. NAGALRO

---

[63] Paras 34, 44
[64] Ev 228
[65] Ev 242 para 2.1
[66] Ev 239
[67] Paras 112 ff

reported to us that, when trying to negotiate with CAFCASS senior management, they often found that answers came back only after consultation with LCD officials.[68]

50. These interventions may have been due to a lack of confidence in the ability of the Board and senior management team to cope with the difficulties being experienced. In view of the comments above, that lack of confidence may well have been justified. Nevertheless it should not be forgotten that it was Ministers who were responsible for the appointment of the Board and the senior management team in the first place.

Suspicions of cost-cutting

51. More broadly, witnesses reported that the LCD's attitude to CAFCASS in those early days appeared to be driven not by a desire to achieve the best possible level of service for children and the courts, but by a desire to keep costs down.[69] This evidence suggested that the level of initial funding which CAFCASS received was due to an inability accurately to record the actual cost of the service and to a desire to keep costs to an absolute minimum. It also suggested that the dispute with the guardians was a part of that cost-cutting agenda. An article published in the New Law Journal at around the time of the dispute sums up this view:

> The conspiratorial view would be that both CAFCASS and the Lord Chancellor's Department would be very happy to have the existing self-employed guardians leave the service. They provide a standard to which neither organisation aspires. They provide a focus for continuing to fight for that standard. Without them it will be easier to reduce the budget …[70]

The subsequent budget increases, rather than disproving the theory, only go to show how short-sighted this attitude was.

Tandem representation

52. Suspicions of a cost-cutting agenda on the part of the Department are reflected in the fears expressed by a number of witnesses about the future of the system of "tandem representation", whereby a child is represented in court by both a solicitor and a children's guardian. Witnesses have felt this system to be under threat, despite the fact that it is much envied in other jurisdictions.[71] All the evidence we have received points to the value of the system and the benefits it brings to vulnerable children. In recognition of those benefits, section 122 of the Adoption and Children Act 2002, when implemented, will for the first time set in primary legislation the power to provide for separate representation in appropriate cases in private law. There was considerable concern that CAFCASS's current difficulties might also delay the implementation of this section, which was very widely welcomed when it was introduced into the Adoption and Children Bill.[72] **The Minister for Children and the CAFCASS Board should make a definitive statement about their**

---

[68] Q 172
[69] Ev 86, 196–197, 217
[70] NLJ Practitioner June 29 2001, page 965
[71] Ev 96, 97, 123 para 3.1, 128–129, 141,188; Q 205 etc
[72] Ev 189 para 14; Q 132

commitment to maintaining a system of tandem representation. These provisions are consistent with Article 12 of the United Nations Convention on the Rights of the Child.[73]

Work of the Project Team

53. We record above the work which was done by working groups and the Project Team in preparation for the establishment of CAFCASS. As the Department's memorandum implies, whilst it may have been envisaged that this work would be taken forward by CAFCASS once established, the written evidence we received suggested that that CAFCASS had in fact failed to make use of the very considerable work done by those groups.[74]

54. Many rumours surrounded the fate of the work that was done, ranging from its deliberate non-use by the senior management team to allegations that Departmental officials had "locked it in a cupboard" and denied the senior management team access to it.[75] We questioned a number of witnesses on the reasons for the failure to make use of this work, without receiving any very satisfactory answers.[76] Perhaps the closest we got to the true explanation of what had happened was the suggestion by the LCD Head of Family Policy Division that the work was "not lost, but lost sight of."[77] The CAFCASS Chairman claimed that in fact the work of the Project Teams *had* been built on and used, and professed himself "quite distressed" that our witnesses had suggested otherwise.[78] However, the Chief Executive's view, that "the momentum of some of this work was lost", appears to us to be closer to an acknowledgement of what really happened.[79] It seems incontrovertible that the work which was done was not properly used in those early days. For an organisation already struggling with the difficulties of an unreasonably truncated time for establishment, to fail even to use the work which was able to be done in the limited time available represents serious mismanagement.

55. The effect of the failure to use that work was not just a practical one in the sense that difficulties which could have been avoided were not avoided and progress which could have been made was not made. It is impossible to tell whether the suggestion made by one of our witnesses—that "there was a cut off point on 1 April 2001 when CAFCASS senior management said 'Right, nothing that has happened before 1 April matters. We can start again'"[80]—is correct or not. There is no doubt, however, that the failure to build on the work done by so many different organisations and experienced practitioners created an

---

[73] Article 12 of the Convention states—

"*States Parties shall assure to the child who is capable of forming his or her own views the right to express those views freely in all matters affecting the child, the views of the child being given due weight in accordance with the age and maturity of the child*"

[74] Ev 119, 129, 152, 167–168, 196–197

[75] Ev 250 (Q 194) para 1.1, 119; NLJ Practitioner Aug 3 2001, page 1160

[76] Qq 3, 174, 192, 210 ff, 217, 232

[77] Q 305

[78] Q 279 ff

[79] Q 281

[80] Q 194

impression that the views of stakeholders were not valued, and that at a time when the Service was in need of all the help it could get.[81]

56. The Project Team cost a considerable amount of money—some £9 million, we were told.[82] The failure to use the work which was done was thus not only a waste of many people's time and effort, but a serious waste of money.

Review by the National Audit Office

57. We have examined events surrounding the establishment and early days of CAFCASS in order to understand the context within which CAFCASS is now working. We have not explored all the details of the problems which were experienced at this time. Nevertheless, our inquiry has produced evidence of the serious mismanagement of the establishment of CAFCASS both before and after vesting day. Considerable amounts of public money were involved and those responsible should be held to account. **We recommend that the National Audit Office review these events, including: use of the work of the Project Team;[83] development of IT systems in CAFCASS[84]; management of senior staff and use of consultants in the early months of CAFCASS; and events surrounding the departures of the Chief Executive and Director of Operations.**

---

[81] Qq 175, 192 ff, 212, 218
[82] Q 193; ev 238
[83] Ev 238–239
[84] Q 236

5 Current situation

58. This chapter of our Report examines the consequences of the failures of CAFCASS's early days, and considers the extent to which the organisation is still suffering from them.

Failures in service provision

59. MCSI's first report on CAFCASS, *Setting Up*, concluded that, despite all the difficulties which were experienced in the early months, front-line services had to a very large extent been maintained.[85] Despite that finding, however, concern grew about delays in the allocation of CAFCASS officers to cases, particularly in public law. By the time of our inquiry, those delays were the main focus of concern amongst witnesses.[86]

60. Delay almost always undermines the welfare of children and the rights of parents and children: a fact recognised in the "no delay" principle underpinning the Children Act. The passage of months whilst decisions are made represents a substantial proportion of their lives. While this process continues, children may be deeply distressed by the fact that they are living in an unfamiliar environment and denied contact with parents, grandparents, brothers or sisters.[87] The courts recognise the importance of stability to children by frequently making decisions which reflect the *status quo*. Therefore delay not only impacts on children's day to day relationships, but also reduces the options available to the courts and risks parents' and children's rights to establish family life together.

61. The precise extent of delay in allocation occurring before the establishment of CAFCASS is not known.[88] Information on case allocation by the pre-existing guardian panels was not centrally collected. However, it can be said that whilst there were some delays in some areas, in others a guardian was typically appointed within 24 hours.[89]

62. The contrast with the situation post-CAFCASS could hardly be greater. Figures provided by the Law Society suggested that, in public law cases, by the time of our inquiry average waiting times for the appointment of a children's guardian were around five working weeks.[90] Recent figures for unallocated cases, supplied to us by CAFCASS, are as follows:[91]

---

[85] *op cit*, Chief Inspector's Foreword
[86] Ev 213, 219, 246–252; Qq 44, 205, 90 [Ms Gieve], 119, 182. See also results of Law Society survey of its Children's Panel completed in March 2003
[87] Q 205 [Mr White]
[88] Ev 124, 234
[89] Ev 247 para 4 viii; Q 181. See also recent Annual Reports of GALRO Panels for, for example, Heart of England, Cumbria, Northamptonshire, Leicestershire and Rutland, South-east Wales, Wiltshire and others
[90] Law Society Children Panel survey, March 2003
[91] The corresponding figures for total live caseloads are:

	March	April	May
Public Law	12480	12270	12077
Private Law	8094	8524	8398

	March	*April*	*May*
Public law[92]	639	576	602
Private law[93]	365	418	399

It is true that these figures conceal significant regional variations. **In some places, there are no significant delays, and the service being provided by CAFCASS is as good as that which was provided by its predecessor service.**[94] **In others, however—inner London, for example—delays have reached wholly unacceptable levels.**[95]

63. The position in private law does not show such a marked deterioration as that in public law; but this is mainly because the pre-CAFCASS situation was already unsatisfactory. Representatives from the Law Society told us that there had been little or no improvement from the position under the old Family Court Welfare Service, where reports would typically take some twelve weeks to complete, and that in some cases the position had got worse.[96]

Reasons for delay

64. As noted by the Minister in her most recent memorandum, the reasons for delay in allocation are complex.[97] There is undoubtedly a higher level of demand than was faced by those services which existed pre-CAFCASS. CAFCASS has recorded a particular increase in care case requests, those cases being the more complex in occurring in public law. There is also an issue concerning the wide variations in the amount of time individual practitioners spend on any one case, which affects the number of cases a practitioner can take in total.[98] The bottom line, however, as the Chief Executive eventually acknowledged,[99] is that CAFCASS has not had sufficient staff resources to cope with the demand it has faced.[100]

65. Again, the reasons for this lack of resources are not straightforward. CAFCASS has been hit by the general shortage of experienced social work staff which is affecting local authority social services departments across the country.[101] Recruitment has not been easy. Furthermore, the dispute with self-employed guardians resulted in a moratorium on recruitment (so as not to prejudice the position of the guardians) whilst the dispute was

---

[92] "Snapshot figure" for unallocated cases. The figures for the number of cases unallocated after 7 days (the time on which the performance target in CAFCASS's Corporate Plan is based) is April 490, May 511 (*figures not available for March*)

[93] Cases unallocated 10 weeks before the filing date with the courts

[94] Qq 47, 51

[95] Ev 95 para 2, 97, 104, 137, 140 para 3.1, 188 para 7, 194–195, etc

[96] Q 90 [Ms Blacklaws, Mr Watson-Lee]

[97] Ev 231

[98] Ev 124–125, 235 para 2.2

[99] Q 265

[100] Q 104; Ev 97, 103 para 5, 137, 141 para 3.7, 151–152, 246–248, etc

[101] Q 104; Ev 89, 101, 141 para 3.7, 187 para 1, 219 para 2

resolved, thus preventing CAFCASS from bringing more people in for a period of some months early in its existence.

66. However, **the increase in demand—which did not start post-CAFCASS[102] and should have been anticipated—and the shortage of appropriately qualified staff made it all the more important that CAFCASS hold on to the staff it was inheriting. The protracted dispute damaged relations with experienced guardians and staff the organisation desperately needed in order properly to fulfil one of its core functions. Key front-line practitioners were lost.**[103]

CAFCASS Legal

67. Concerns have also been expressed about the work of CAFCASS Legal. The head of this part of CAFCASS seems to be widely held in very high regard.[104] Nonetheless CAFCASS Legal appears to be suffering from the same lack of staff as is affecting other parts of CAFCASS. A number of witnesses reported to us that CAFCASS Legal now seemed unable to take on cases which its predecessor, the Children's Division of the Official Solicitor, would have been expected to handle.[105] The President of the Family Division expressed concern that CAFCASS Legal was both "seriously under-resourced for lawyers" and "very short of case workers."[106]

Lowering of standards for recruitment

68. Once CAFCASS was able to start recruiting again, it reacted to the shortage of available staff by lowering the required level of experience from 5 years to three. A number of witnesses expressed concern to us about this, arguing that there was evidence of a lowering of standards of work and, in some cases, a failure on the part of new guardians to understand what role they ought properly to be playing in proceedings.[107] CAFCASS itself denied that there was any lowering of standards, and the representatives of the judiciary who appeared before us mostly considered that the standard of work they saw was as good as it had ever been.[108] Representatives of the CAFCASS Managers Association were also at pains to defend the quality of work done by their staff, even new recruits.[109] However, one of the representatives of the judiciary, Judge Crichton from the Inner London Family Proceedings Court, suggested that he was now seeing some work of an unacceptable standard.[110] There were also reports from some lawyers who work closely with children's guardians of new guardians who were not fully aware of the proper role to be played by a children's guardian.[111] Some of these instances may have been the result of CAFCASS

---

[102] See Judicial Statistics Annual Reports

[103] See the results of a recent survey by the guardians' professional association NAGALRO, which shows a dramatic drop in self-employed guardians' availability for CAFCASS work since April 2001 (available on www.nagalro.com)

[104] Q 77

[105] Ev 86 para 8, 179; Qq 77, 98

[106] Q 77

[107] Ev 91, 116 para 31, 120, 121, 159, 175 para 20, 177 para 7, 219 s 3; Qq 19, 162, 208

[108] Q 65 ff

[109] Q 228

[110] Q 68

[111] Qq 68, 90 [Ms Blacklaws], 162, 208. See also Q 19

finding itself obliged to resort to the use of agency staff to try to tackle the growing crisis in allocation of guardians in London.[112]

Training

69. The evidence we have received suggests that lower standards of work, where they occur, are due as much to the lack of training and professional development in CAFCASS as to inappropriate recruitment.[113] A lack of a properly structured and quality-assured training programme, or of any organised professional development activity, was a common complaint in evidence, particularly that coming from guardians.[114]

70. Pre-CAFCASS, guardians could expect regular sessions of training and professional development.[115] Panel Committees were responsible for overseeing the training of panel members.[116] Panel managers and panel members arranged induction training for new guardians, including shadowing experienced practitioners, guardians held regular professional meetings to provide mutual advice and support, and seminars were organised on specific topics often involving social workers and lawyers and other professionals.[117] Guardian panels would often pay self-employed guardians to attend such events. Family court welfare officers employed by the Probation Service also enjoyed organised training and development. They could have expected a period of induction training on moving into court welfare work, regular supervision from the Senior Family Court Welfare Officer, and team-based and regional staff development exercises. Many court welfare teams used a variety of methods of working together with colleagues to monitor and improve their skills, usually with the aim of updating each other and developing best practice.

71. Yet even pre-existing arrangements have not been continued. A memorandum from a group of self-employed guardians in the south-west of England compares the situation pre-CAFCASS with that which obtains now:

> Until April 2002 there was a great deal of professional support and structure in place for self-employed guardians in our area to keep our practice safe. The emphasis was on developing professional judgement. Since Cafcass took over the service the emphasis for practitioners has been on meeting organisational demands. Now, we only have Business Meetings once every two months, and these meetings do not address professional issues or facilitate case discussion. We used to have monthly Professional Development Meetings but these meetings are no longer available. There has been minimal effort to get self-employed and employed Guardians harmonised with one another and together to discuss professional issues. Liaison between old and new Guardians is not properly facilitated [and] therefore does not

---

[112] Ev 236 para 4
[113] Ev 189 para 18
[114] Ev 84, 93, 129 ff, 136, 157, 159, 178 para 15, 245 para 15, 252, 229 para 6.4; Qq 4, 103, 132, 134 [Ms Leach], 163, 233
[115] Qq 162 [Miss Edwards], 164 [Mr Griffith-Jones]
[116] The Guardian ad litem and Reporting Officers (Panels) Regulations 1991 (S.I 1991 No 2051) para 8(c)
[117] See, for example, ev 213 para 7

happen, resulting in previous practice and experience not being shared and built upon between old and new Guardians, creating a great divide ...[118]

Only during our questioning of the Chief Executive did it emerge that self-employed guardians were finally to be granted access to the CAFCASS intranet.[119] We have even been told that CAFCASS management has attempted to discourage use amongst CAFCASS practitioners of an e-mail 'smartgroup' which has been operating as a forum for good practice, exchange of information and professional development.[120] The short-sightedness of such an attitude is self-evident.

Consequences of the lack of training

72. One of the consequences of the failure to provide proper training was the poor preparation of new recruits for their role, which we discuss above.[121] Another was the reinforcement of the impression that CAFCASS as an organisation did not value its professional practitioners. The following comment, from Ms K Butcher, a children's guardian, is typical:

> The loss of quality is underpinned by the lack of training, appraisals and learning from each other within the organisation. As a self-employed Guardian I am not expected to contribute to the development of the service. My expertise is under valued and under used...[122]

73. The consequences are not confined to individual CAFCASS practitioners. The training and professional development of CAFCASS practitioners is a vital part of the development and improvement of the service given to children and the courts. Evidence from court users, notably non-resident parents groups and those representing women who have suffered from domestic violence, emphasised the importance to CAFCASS officers of a proper understanding of the context within which they are working, and full awareness of the relevant research.[123] If this is not the case, vulnerable children may suffer too.

Convergence

74. Particular concerns were expressed in this context about 'convergence', i.e. the process of enabling children's guardians to do the work of family court welfare officers, and vice versa. The original intention of CAFCASS was to bring together the work in public and private law, in order to achieve both efficiency savings and cross-fertilisation of ideas.[124] However, while many of the skills are transferable, the tasks of representing and reporting are substantially different and require specialist areas of knowledge.[125] Children's guardians and others expressed considerable concern about convergence and the failure of CAFCASS

---

[118] Ev 159
[119] Q 286
[120] Ev 93, 229 para 6.4
[121] Para 68
[122] Ev 84; see also Ev 91 para 2, 135 s 2, 165 para 4.15, etc
[123] Ev 70, 79, 82, 252, etc
[124] Government consultation paper *Support Services in family* proceedings, *op cit*. See also Ev 127 para 29
[125] Ev 127 para 30; Q132

properly to appreciate the difference between the respective roles.[126] The children's guardian Veronica Swenson, for example, says,

> The latest attempt at an 'Induction Training Course' fails to distinguish between the discrete functions of robust independent scrutiny (identifying and protecting children's interests) and of helping parties move toward agreement (settling adults' disputes). This typifies the confused, bungling way in which CAFCASS conflates professional roles…[127]

75. CAFCASS appears not to have taken sufficient account of these concerns. There has been very little development of training to enable the two strands of professionals to develop the skills needed to undertake both sides of the work.[128] Indeed, until recently there has been virtually no development of training of any kind. Yet CAFCASS is already advertising for the recruitment of generic "family court advisers", who will be expected to undertake both roles, and issuing "harmonised" contracts to existing staff.[129] As Joan Hunt of Oxford University points out in her discussion of the desire to make progress on convergence, "it [is] very clear that a substantial programme of training and support [is] absolutely vital… It is doubtful whether Cafcass is in a position to do this properly at the moment."[130]

Performance management and appraisal

76. An associated issue is that of performance management and appraisal. One of the reasons for the establishment of CAFCASS was the feeling that the pre-existing guardian panels were able to exercise insufficient control over the cost-effectiveness and value for money offered by guardians in their area.[131] CAFCASS appears to have responded to that concern not by strengthening the appraisal system, but by attempting to impose what were seen as rigid constraints on the work guardians can do on a case (as detailed elsewhere in this Report[132]). In the meantime, the system of professional support and performance management has disappeared.[133] It may be that this is in some measure due to the fact that front-line team managers, who might be expected to carry out appropriate appraisal of the work of the practitioners they manage, are too busy to be able to do so.[134] Other witnesses suggested that many front-line managers simply do not have the public law expertise to be able to make the judgements required.[135] Front-line practitioners very much regret the lack of professional support which CAFCASS is offering them.

---

[126] Ev 194 s 4; Qq 47, 107, 132, 133, 145, 165
[127] Ev 130
[128] Ev 68 para 12, 255, 256
[129] Q 275
[130] Ev 127 para 30
[131] See para 16 above
[132] Paras 36 ff
[133] Ev 85, 136 para 3, 219–220 ss 5 and 6, 239; Qq 160, 220
[134] Q 233
[135] Ev 93 para 13, 36 para 3, 98 para 3.4; Q 95

Information Technology

77. The conclusion of MCSI in its first report on CAFCASS, *Setting Up*, was that "IT was a CAFCASS success story."[136] The experience of CAFCASS staff working with the existing systems, however, does not appear to concur with that conclusion.

78. CAFCASS's main failure in respect of IT is the lack of a case management system. The need for such a system, which would enable the collection and retrieval of up-to-date information on cases with which CAFCASS is involved, was identified early on in the planning for the establishment of CAFCASS. At setup, a large sum of money—some £6m, we were told—was provided for the development of IT systems in CAFCASS. We were told that work on a case management system had begun during the pre-CAFCASS period,[137] but that it had stopped shortly after CAFCASS was formally established because the project managers feared that it would fall prey to the same problems which have beset many other public sector IT projects.[138] It is not clear what then happened to the money which had been provided for the establishment of the system.[139]

79. Since work on the project was halted, minimal progress has been made on the development of appropriate IT systems. New hardware has been delivered to offices, and is used for word processing, e-mail and other office applications. Crucially, however, there is still no software available which will enable this new hardware to manage and share information about live cases. Instead, staff are still working with the different legacy systems inherited from the previous services. Information thus has to be laboriously transferred from one system to another to provide statistics demanded by management. Not only does this result in large amounts of extra work having to be done by front-line management and administrative staff, but questions also have to be raised about the robustness of the information received in this way by regional and national management. Even if mistakes are not made, there can be no guarantee that the information is sufficiently up-to-date for the purposes required.[140]

80. A further consequence of the failure to establish an appropriate case management system is CAFCASS's inability to collect information for research and evaluation purposes.[141] The information collected on the legacy systems is, in most cases, very basic. It does not, for instance, enable information to be gathered on repeat litigation: whether parties come back to court again after one set of proceedings has been completed, how many times they do so, and how long after the original proceedings. Information such as this could be used to judge the success or otherwise of different approaches to dealing with private law disputes. We describe below the importance of research in this area of work, and the lack of it.[142] Yet two years of potentially valuable data relating to practice have been

---

[136] *op cit*, p 14

[137] Q 234

[138] Qq 37, 281

[139] Ev 139 s 3(a); Q 236

[140] Ev 102 para 10, 125 para 13 and 240–241; Qq 39 ff

[141] Qq 9, 39, 220

[142] Para 93 ff

lost because no appropriate means of collecting them have been developed.[143] This is a major missed opportunity.

Support services

81. There were high hopes when CAFCASS was created that it would provide new services to support the courts, especially in private law cases. Such services might include contact centres, mediation, parent education, and other support services for parents and children post-separation and divorce. Considerable play was made of the inclusion of an additional 'S' in the CAFCASS acronym that added the support function to its title.

82. A Report prepared last year by the LCD's Advisory Board on Family Law: Children Act Sub-Committee, *Making Contact Work*, saw an expanded CAFCASS as of "critical importance" to the development of additional support services for families suffering breakdown. The report suggested that if CAFCASS could achieve this role there would be not only improved outcomes for the families concerned, but also significant savings in time and money to the family court system.[144] Witnesses to our inquiry have echoed comments about the vital role which CAFCASS could and should play outside the formal court processes.[145]

83. The evidence we have received, however, suggests that CAFCASS is very far from getting to grips with the central role envisaged for it in *Making Contact Work*. Considerable disappointment is expressed that such support services have not been provided and that even existing measures, such as family assistance orders, are seldom recommended or used because of resource considerations.[146] The main reason for this failure is that CAFCASS quite simply does not have enough staff resources to be able to cope with such an expansion of its role. However, evidence also suggested that CAFCASS is in a poor position to develop support services and has no clear policy about such developments, reflecting uncertainty about the role and function of CAFCASS in relation to this aspect of its remit.[147] CAFCASS's strategic role in the provision of support services was not clear: the question of whether it or the LCD was best placed to play the coordinating role in the development of such services was never satisfactorily answered.

Partnership funding

84. Currently, CAFCASS's main contribution to additional support services comes through the £1.1m (slightly more than 1% of its total budget) which it provides in "partnership funding" for other organisations, chiefly those who provide contact centres and mediation services.[148] CAFCASS has recently announced a decision to "rebalance" that money so that more of it goes to contact centres, and less to mediation services (which, it argues, receive substantial funding from elsewhere).[149] This decision suggests that

---

[143] Ev 239; Q 9
[144] Available at http://www.lcd.gov.uk/family/abfla/mcwrep.htm
[145] Ev 152, 252
[146] Ev 83–84, 88, 97, 177, 241 para 1.3, 252; Qq 86 ff, 214; etc
[147] Ev 242 para 1.9; Qq 28, 107 and 132
[148] Ev 110 final table
[149] *Partnership Strategy Consultation: Final Report*, CAFCASS, February 2003

CAFCASS feels a need to focus quite narrowly on 'in-court' conciliation work and the funding of contact centres, leaving the development of wider support work to others.

85. This may be an understandable position to take in the short term, and defensible on its own terms.[150] Nevertheless the decision to reduce funding for mediation rather seems to contrast with CAFCASS's stated belief that "the best interests of children may be better served, in private law cases, by taking more action to avoid cases coming to ... court".[151] Contact centres, although very necessary and valuable, can of course only deal with the effects of arrangements that have already been made, either through court or independently; unlike mediation services, they cannot prevent cases coming to court in the first place.

86. Fears have also been expressed that the withdrawal of CAFCASS funding from not-for-profit mediation services will result in the loss of some of those services altogether.[152] Whether that is the case or not—and notwithstanding the satisfaction with which the decision will doubtless have been received by those representing contact centres, many of which are run on a shoestring—the decision comes as a great disappointment to those who saw CAFCASS as a major developer of a range of support services for families experiencing breakdown.

Effect of LCD's PSA targets

87. We note in passing that the LCD has as one of its PSA targets "to increase the level of contact between children and non-resident parents, where that is in the best interests of the child." We express elsewhere in this Report concerns about the relationship between LCD and CAFCASS.[153] There is speculation that CAFCASS has felt the need to focus on child contact because that may be the only way the Department can meet its targets. If true, this would indicate a degree of short-sightedness on the part of both LCD and CAFCASS, which we hope will not be replicated by the DfES.

Relations with the Legal Services Commission

88. Relations with the Legal Services Commission (LSC) are crucial in the context of development of support services. The LSC occasionally funds assessments for contact and funds contracted mediation providers by paying for mediation for those who qualify for public funding (i.e. on a means tested basis). It is also running a pilot project, FAInS (Family Advice and Information Services), which is designed to ensure access to tailored information and advice for those who are contemplating or who have decided on separation or divorce. There is therefore an important link between the work of the two organisations.

89. There is little evidence that CAFCASS and the Legal Services Commission have so far been working together in partnership to ensure a coordinated approach to the provision of appropriate services. A number of comments from CAFCASS's recent review of its

---

[150] *ibid*
[151] CAFCASS Corporate Plan 2003–06, p 30
[152] Ev 211 para 20, 222 para 4.6
[153] Para 112 ff

partnership arrangements with other organisations serve to illustrate the approach which appears to be being taken:

> LSC views contact centre funding as largely CAFCASS business…
>
> Some CAFCASS managers have expressed anxiety over possible 'double funding' of mediation, given inherited arrangements and the relatively large sums now provided by the LSC and want CAFCASS mediation funding reviewed.
>
> One of the difficulties in ensuring value for money when contracting with child contact centres and mediation services is that funding frequently works to support or subsidise other referrers and there is not a direct benefit to CAFCASS……solicitors typically make 50% or more of contact centre referrals.[154]

90. In particular, considerable cooperation might have been expected between the two organisations on the FAInS project. Yet the "bidding document" which preceded the establishment of that project made no mention of CAFCASS, despite CAFCASS's key role in this area. Para 5.5 of the LSC's memorandum makes it clear that LSC do not propose to involve CAFCASS directly in the FAInS project.[155] As the memorandum from Parentline Plus and the National Council for One Parent Families, for example, points out, "it is vital that CAFCASS employees are able to signpost parents and families onto appropriate national and locally based sources of information, help and support."[156] Working with families who are likely to make use of such information services is central to CAFCASS's *raison d'être*.

Relations with other organisations

91. Evidence from Napo, one of the trade unions representing CAFCASS staff, suggested a certain amount of difficulty was being experienced by CAFCASS practitioners in accessing information from other agencies about individuals involved in proceedings. A survey of 60 practitioners, in which each was asked to report on their last five cases, found that "whilst the vast majority of the respondents were able to access data fairly quickly and easily, there were 74 instances where difficulties were experienced with one of more of the key departments." They concluded that "these difficulties with other agencies underline a need for national protocols to be developed."[157]

92. These are important findings, albeit based on a relatively small sample. Perhaps more seriously, the CAFCASS Managers Association suggested that many front-line managers were having to withdraw from liaison arrangements with, for example, the courts and local authorities, through simple pressure of overwork.[158] As well as potentially contributing to the problems of data-sharing described by Napo—good working relationships need commitment on both sides—such withdrawal bodes ill for the inter-agency cooperation which is essential in the context of child protection, as the Victoria Climbié inquiry has

---

[154] *Partnership Strategy: A Consultation* Paper, CAFCASS, October 2002. See also Ev 242 para 1.6; Qq 111 ff
[155] Ev 223 para 5.5
[156] Ev 89 para 11
[157] Ev 156 para 12. See also qq 139 ff
[158] Ev 239; Q 220

most recently stressed. **Full involvement by all concerned, CAFCASS staff included, in inter-agency initiatives and joint working is essential if disasters such as the Victoria Climbié affair are to be avoided in future.**

Research and improving practice

93. The formation of a unified service should have provided the opportunity for a concerted effort on the part of those working in the family justice system to develop a strategy for addressing some important unanswered questions about "what works" for children following family breakdown. As with so many other areas, however, it is an opportunity which CAFCASS has not yet managed to grasp.

94. MCSI's latest report on CAFCASS says:

> Given the relative paucity of research in recent years into areas covered by CAFCASS, a great deal of catching up is needed. MCSI believes that CAFCASS needs to develop a strategy for knowledge accrual, including research, focusing on the 'what works' approach to family proceedings related work. This should include establishing clear links with relevant research foundations such as, for example, Nuffield, Rowntree and the Economic and Social Research Council (ESRC), as well as university based researchers and research units in the central Government departments.[159]

This conclusion elicited from CAFCASS itself the rather weak response, "We will ensure practice is evidence based and supported by a strategy for research, best practice and quality assurance."[160]

95. The importance of research to the process of determining what is "in the best interests of the child" can hardly be overstated. The Children Act 1989, s.1, expressly requires the court to give paramount consideration to the welfare of the child. Far greater attempts are made than was once the case to link decisions with expert understandings of child development and children's well-being. However, 'evidence-based practice', which is of growing importance in areas such as health and social care, is lacking, particularly in the area of the management of private law disputes and decisions about contact. The complaints which we have received from non-resident parents and their representative groups alleging bias against them on the part of CAFCASS, for example, perhaps reflect the concern expressed by MCSI that CAFCASS is to some extent working in a vacuum when it comes to making recommendations to a court about what is going to be best for any particular child.

96. **The ability of CAFCASS to evaluate the outcomes of its interventions—in other words, to identify 'what works' and to develop best practice accordingly—depends in part upon the development of a reliable data base that can be submitted to rigorous and detailed analysis.** In the absence of such data, the identification of what might be best for any particular child in any particular case is fraught with difficulty. **The development of a research-friendly culture, which welcomes external analysis and can work in**

---

[159] *Setting a Course*, para 2.48. See also Q 9, and Ev 239
[160] *ibid*, page 45

partnership with the research community, will be central to the achievement of this goal.

6 Corporate governance

97. Many of the concerns we have discussed earlier in this report may be put down to the difficulties inherent in creating a new organisation to take over the running of services previously provided by a number of others. The evidence we have received, however, suggests that the task of creating that new service has been hampered not merely by those inherent difficulties, but by more fundamental failures in management, organisation and corporate governance. We touch on those concerns above: in this chapter we discuss them more fully.

Management and organisational culture

98. CAFCASS's strapline, which appears on all its documents, says, *"Putting children and young people first"*. However, evidence not only from children's guardians but also from solicitors, voluntary organisations and CAFCASS's own managers has suggested that from its inception CAFCASS at a national level has given greater consideration to its own corporate priorities than to promoting and defending the interests of children.[161]

Management

99. A number of witnesses suggested that CAFCASS was over-managed.[162] We were told that the ratio of managers to practitioners had increased markedly since CAFCASS's establishment. CAFCASS has an extensive management hierarchy, comprising four tiers of managers below the Board (Chief Executive, Director of Operations, Regional Manager, Team Manager). The CAFCASS Board has recently approved proposals to add in an extra tier, Divisional Manager, directly below Director of Operations.[163] This contrasts with the "flat" management structure envisaged by many when CAFCASS was established.[164]

100. Allegations of "top-heavy" management sit side-by-side with suggestions from other witnesses—notably, for instance, the CAFCASS Managers' Association—that there is a dearth of front-line managers, and that CAFCASS does not have a sufficiently rigorous performance management system in place to monitor, manage and improve the performance of front-line staff.[165] They also sit uneasily beside MCSI's conclusion that management capacity at headquarters needed to be strengthened.[166]

101. One way of explaining this paradox might be to return to the allegation of excessive attention to corporate priorities. CAFCASS has had to develop management structures for a completely new organisation, which is no easy task. Many have seen CAFCASS as devoting disproportionate attention to devising and implementing management structures, at the expense of consideration of how to improve its service to children and the

---

[161] Ev 141 para 3.8, 198 para 4.1, 212 para 23, 217, 239, 244 para 2; Qq 124 [Ms Timms], 127, 157 ff, 190, etc
[162] Ev 83, 85, 102 para 9, 112, 119,121; Qq 158, 221
[163] CAFCASS Board Minutes for 5 March 2003, item 9 (available on www.cafcass.gov.uk), Q 221
[164] Ev 112 para 12, 166 para 6.4 f, 250 para 2.2. See also Ev 198 para 3.1
[165] Ev 136 s 3, 219 s 3; Q220. See also para 76 above
[166] *Setting a Course*, para 2.22

courts. The decision to introduce yet another tier of management is but the latest example of this. In the light of the findings set out elsewhere in this Report, the strengthening of management capacity at Headquarters recommended by MCSI might better be achieved by the recruitment of more policy development and research staff. A more telling explanation for the complaints about management style comes in a submission from a CAFCASS Board member.

102. Our witness comments, "the evidence given to the Select Committee has been that there continues to be real dissatisfaction with the management style of the organisation. It is regarded as centralist, hierarchical and demanding, while still struggling in areas to get its own act together. The enormous resources of talent and experience among the local workforces often seem not to be effectively used."[167]

103. She continues,

> I believe the reality is that CAFCASS management are developing a fairly standard central control management style and structure. This is partly because that is what they are comfortable and familiar with and partly because the external demands for information and response appear to imply a top down hierarchy and centrally imposed national standardisation.
>
> Management are, I believe, distinctly uncomfortable and critical of the pre CAFCASS Guardian approach which allowed practitioners to self manage on a professional basis and respond to the demands of the court system on an individual basis while working to a panel with no budgetary control.
>
> I am confident that there is another way to manage the organisation using a more bottom up creative approach and that this would create an organisation which was more enjoyable to work in and achieved more while still delivering the overall management of the organisation. However there is no experience at senior management level in CAFCASS or the LCD of this approach and therefore there is neither the vision, expertise or will to try and implement it.[168]

Internal communications and relations with front-line staff

104. Despite the emphasis on management structures, CAFCASS has failed to establish effective links between Headquarters and front-line staff on the ground. MCSI found that "some staff [at headquarters] saw no relevance to their particular jobs in being informed about how front-line services were delivered."[169] On the public law side, the dearth of managers at all levels with knowledge and experience of public law exacerbated the difficulties which were bound to occur in the move from the lightly-managed GALRO Panels to the more formal line-managed structure of the new service. Poor internal communications have alienated front-line practitioners and created a very difficult working environment for front-line managers and administrative staff.[170] There is ample

---

[167] Ev 228
[168] Ev 229
[169] *Setting a Course*, para 2.32
[170] Ev 139, 239

evidence of the failure of internal communications in the conflicting accounts of the Chief Executive, on the one hand, and the CAFCASS Managers' Association, on the other, concerning promulgation of the announcement of our inquiry.[171]

105. The consequences of the failure to understand the needs, feelings and concerns of front-line staff—both managers and practitioners—or how the service actually works have had an effect on many different areas of CAFCASS's work. The most obvious example of the failure of management to address the needs of staff and the Service is the dispute with self-employed guardians, which we discuss above.[172] We have not examined in detail the claim and counter-claim which has surrounded this unfortunate episode in CAFCASS's development. We have not, therefore, taken a view on whether one witness's description of the dispute as "[betraying] a 'Thomas à Beckett' attitude—'who will rid me of these troublesome guardians'"[173]—is justified or not. Whether or not this and similar views are justified, they are certainly widely held,[174] and this in itself is testament to the way in which relations with this important sector of staff have been mishandled. But the evidence which we have received from Napo and, most particularly, from the CAFCASS Managers' Association shows that the problem has affected all parts of the workforce.[175]

The "mixed economy"

106. The decision not to offer self-employment also betrayed an inability to comprehend the nature of the service CAFCASS was supposed to be delivering. In a demand-led service, it seems self-evident that the use of a "pool" of workers who can be called upon when needed, but who do not need to be kept fully employed, is the most effective way of coping with fluctuations in demand.[176] This did not, however, seem to be evident to the CAFCASS Board, advised by the senior management team at the time, when it decided not to offer any self-employed contracts at all. It was this reaction to the dispute over the terms of the self-employed contract which convinced guardians, and many others, that CAFCASS was not interested in achieving the best possible service for the courts and for children; but was rather intent on exercising the greatest possible degree of control over its practitioners.

107. The dispute with guardians made a significant contribution to the problems of delay and the backlog of work which has built up in public law. As a result of the judicial review, a moratorium had to be placed on further recruitment whilst the dispute was settled, preventing CAFCASS from getting in the staff it needed to meet demand for its services. However, the attitude which CAFCASS seemed to be displaying towards its self-employed staff also resulted in the alienation of this group and a perception that they were undervalued. Many left the service altogether and took up other employment in the social work arena. But we were also told that those who remained felt an understandable reluctance to display the same level of commitment to the service as a whole (as opposed to the individual cases on which they were working) which they might have displayed in

---

[171] Ev 239; Q 252
[172] Para 35 ff
[173] Ev 250 para 2.2
[174] See para 38
[175] Ev 137, 153 ff; Qq 136 ff, 216 ff
[176] Ev 93 para 10, 182 para 5; Q 124

similar circumstances pre-CAFCASS.[177] Backlogs and delays in allocation were not unknown under the pre-existing guardian panels. Witnesses told us, however, that the *esprit de corps* amongst the guardian panels would prompt a concerted effort on the part of all concerned to clear any backlog, if necessary by practitioners taking on additional work over and above what they would normally expect to do. In the light of the way they felt they had been treated, guardians working for CAFCASS, it was suggested, decided that it was up to management to find a way out of the hole it had dug for itself. If CAFCASS is concerned, therefore, that over-reliance on self-employed guardians has "inherent risks",[178] it is only because it has not done enough to ensure that self-employed guardians are committed to working for it.

108. Despite the reversal of the decision not to offer self-employed contracts, and the eventual agreement of a suitable contract for self-employed practitioners, guardians have continued to feel that CAFCASS is not fully committed to operating a "mixed economy". They have suggested that the obsession with management remains, often to the detriment of the service. For example, there were allegations:

- that the change in the means of paying travel costs discouraged guardians from working with children now resident some way away, even where the guardian had worked with them before;[179]

- that CAFCASS would not take telephone messages or pass on correspondence for self-employed guardians;[180]

- that self-employed guardians were denied access to the CAFCASS Intranet;[181]

- that self-employed guardians were effectively denied access to training opportunities (because, unlike employed staff, and in contrast to the pre-existing GALRO panels, CAFCASS does not pay its self-employed contractors to attend training)[182].

- that, despite the general shortage of guardians, CAFCASS managers had preferred employed staff over self-employed guardians when allocating cases, even where a self-employed guardian had acted for a child previously. Investigations by MCSI did not substantiate those claims, but did lead to a recommendation that "CAFCASS needs to be able to demonstrate a degree of transparency in implementing its allocation procedures in support of a mixed economy."[183]

109. Even during the course of our inquiry concerns have continued to be raised about the extent of management commitment to the "mixed economy".[184] A supplementary memorandum to our inquiry by CAFCASS notes that the budget provides for the recruitment of a further 132 whole time equivalent practitioners. It says, "Mostly this will

---

[177] Ev 91; Q 156. See also NAGALRO survey of Guardian availability, referred to at note 103 above
[178] Ev 235 para 2.2
[179] Ev 103 para 9. See also Ev 245 paras 12–14
[180] Ev 104
[181] Ev 85, 229 para 6.4
[182] Ev 120–121
[183] *Setting a Course*, para 2.98. See also Ev 245 para 14, 250 para 1.2; Q 160 [Mrs Paddle], Q 224
[184] Ev 248 para 5(ii); Qq 122, 155

be used to recruit employed staff, but some may be used to purchase the services of self-employed practitioners".[185] This does not appear to demonstrate a wholehearted commitment to the mixed economy, notwithstanding the somewhat half-hearted claim to the contrary earlier in the memo.[186] A memorandum from a group of self-employed guardians in the south-west of England, for example, expresses concern at "the number of employed professionals that has recently been recruited in our area, and the ensuing risk that we will be excluded from the service completely."[187]

110. Indeed evidence suggests that CAFCASS senior management still has not grasped the principles of the operation of a "mixed economy". An interview with the Chief Executive, in February this year, records him as saying, "To some extent, unallocated cases are a fact of life. Unless there are a number of staff doing nothing at any one point, there will be requests coming in that have not been allocated."[188] Yet the very point about operating a "mixed economy" is precisely that it is possible to have a number of practitioners, if not "doing nothing", then at least not fully occupied and therefore available to take on new cases. This was how the pre-existing GALRO panels operated, and, whilst delays and backlogs were not unknown, the position never reached the proportions of the current crisis.

111. **It is important that, as well as using and developing its employed guardians, CAFCASS senior management embrace the principle of a mixed economy and repair relations with self-employed guardians.** This is so for a number of reasons. It is not just a question of good staff relations, important though they are. **It would be unacceptable if some children and families were offered an inferior service because of the neglect of a significant part of the skilled available workforce.** If self-employed guardians do not have access to training and professional development, it is difficult to see how they can be expected to provide the optimum level of service to CAFCASS's clients. Just as importantly, however, the effective operation of a mixed economy of employed and self-employed practitioners would make a considerable contribution to the management of the fluctuating demand for CAFCASS's services, and thereby help to reduce the damaging delays in allocation which have been experienced since CAFCASS's establishment.

Relationship between LCD and CAFCASS

112. The starting point for a discussion of the relationship between CAFCASS and the LCD is an understanding of the proper position of a non-departmental public body (NDPB) vis-à-vis its parent Department. According to the Cabinet Office *Classification Guidance*, the purpose of setting up a body as an NDPB is "to permit a service or function to be carried out at arms length from the Government."[189] CAFCASS is constituted by an independent Board made up of a Chairman and not less than ten other members. The Board is appointed by the Lord Chancellor, but the Chief Executive is answerable to the

---

[185] Ev 237 para 5.1
[186] *op cit*, para 2.3(c)
[187] Ev 159
[188] Interview with Jonathan Tross, *childRIGHT*, 12 February 2003
[189] Available on www.cabinet-office.gov.uk

Board, not to a Minister in the sponsoring Department (as is the case, for example, with an executive agency).

113. The decision to establish CAFCASS as an NDPB, rather than an as executive agency or any one of the other options put forward in the 1998 consultation paper, appears to have reflected the views of the majority of respondents to that consultation.[190] The Parliamentary Secretary in the LCD at the time stressed the importance of "making a separation between the developers of family law policy and a service advising the court on the welfare of children."[191]

114. It does not appear, however, that the relationship which has obtained between CAFCASS and the LCD has respected the principles of how an NDPB should be operated. The problem starts with the Framework Document which is supposed to establish the constitutional relationship between CAFCASS and its parent Department. In an important memorandum to this inquiry, Peter Harris, former Official Solicitor, makes a powerful case, which we accept, that **the Framework Document fails to reflect the proper relationship between the LCD and CAFCASS as established by the relevant legislation**.[192] Amongst a number of issues he raises regarding the framework document, the following two are perhaps of most significance:

- the framework document puts a duty on the Chairman of CAFCASS in *advising* the Lord Chancellor on the appointment of a Chief Executive, whereas the statute makes clear that it is the CAFCASS Board which appoints the Chief Executive, albeit only with the approval of the Lord Chancellor;[193]

- a number of statements in section 2.7 of the framework document cannot be reconciled with the statutory basis on which CAFCASS is established, and appear to show the Department assuming greater powers over CAFCASS than is consistent with its position as an NDPB.[194]

115. The degree of dependence on the LCD is evident throughout the document: see, for example, para. 2.2.1, where it is explicitly stated that the "Chairman and Board of CAFCASS are accountable to the Lord Chancellor'"; 2.6.1., where the Lord Chancellor appoints the Chairman; 2.9.1 where the "sponsoring team" is referred to; 3.1.1., where the regularity of meetings between the Chair and the Lord Chancellor is laid down; 4.1.2., where it is stated that the Lord Chancellor "has approved the…key objectives for CAFCASS"; 4.1.3., where the Lord Chancellor agrees the key performance targets and indicators; 5.2.1., where the Lord Chancellor "will inform CAFCASS of his strategic policy objectives"; and so on.

116. Whilst similar requirements may appear in operating documents of other NDPBs, generally such documents are much looser and emphasise the independent role of the NDPB.[195] CAFCASS's Framework Document, whilst not being identical to other

---

[190] Ev 145 para 6.1
[191] Stg Co Deb, Standing Committee G, *Criminal Justice and Court Services Bill*, Tuesday 11 April 2000
[192] Ev 113–115
[193] Ev 114, para 23
[194] Ev 114, para 24
[195] See, for example, the Sustainable Development Commission

framework documents for agencies, bears marked similarities in most respects.[196] The intention to integrate CAFCASS with the work of the Department at all stages is evident throughout the document and belies the claim of NDPB status. Indeed, in his foreword to the document, the Lord Chancellor even refers to the Service as an "agency".

117. **The Framework Document also displays a curious, and worrying, lack of attention to CAFCASS's key role**. Peter Harris describes the problem:

> The framework document which sets out the relationships and responsibilities of the Lord Chancellor, the Board and the Chief Executive, runs to some 42 A4 sheets. It refers to children and advice to the court in paragraph 1.2.2, which in effect reproduces section 12(1) of the Criminal Justice and Court Services Act 2000. One has to turn to Annex A, at page 30, to find a further reference to children and assisting the courts. There is no mention of a duty to "promote the welfare of children who are the subject of family proceedings by the provision of welfare reports to the court", which was seen by Ministers as of central concern in the Consultation Paper, nor of "ensuring that, wherever possible, their [children's] wishes and feelings are placed before the court in accordance with the principles of the UN Convention on the Rights of the Child, particularly Article 12," or that "where rules of court allow, children with party status have a recognised role in the proceedings. This is achieved by representation and should be facilitated by the unified service. ...." These are surely the reasons for bringing the Service into being, and while mention of section 12 of the Act gives the statutory description of functions, a more explicit explanation of what the Service is essentially about should be set out in the framework document.[197]

118. Peter Harris's conclusions are supported by a number of other witnesses.[198] It is interesting also to compare them with MCSI's suggestion that, "the LCD might wish to reconsider, in the light of the findings of its Departmental Landscape Review, whether NDPB status is optimal for this organisation":[199] a suggestion which the Chief Inspector later clarified as meaning reconstituting CAFCASS as an executive agency, rather than an NDPB.[200] In the light of the other evidence we have received, it seems that this suggestion goes less to a change in the relationship between CAFCASS and the LCD than to reflecting formally the position which currently obtains.

119. The full extent to which the resulting confusion contributed to the problems which CAFCASS has experienced, particularly the dispute with self-employed guardians, is difficult to judge. The impression grew amongst guardians and others that the LCD exercised control behind the scenes over decisions about the guardian service.[201] **CAFCASS provides a vitally important service in which we would expect Ministers to take a close interest. The confusion over the terms on which they do so has resulted from the unclear constitutional relationship between LCD and CAFCASS. It has produced**

---

[196] See, for example, framework documents for the Prisons Agency, the Appeals Service, or the NHS Purchasing Agency
[197] Ev 114 para 20
[198] Ev 181 para 14, 192 para 2.1.3; Q 173. See also *Setting a Course*, para 2.3
[199] *Setting a Course, op cit*, paras 2.25–26
[200] Ev 220–221
[201] Ev 242 s 2

suspicions of inappropriate interference and has hampered efforts to establish a properly functioning service.[202] The resolution of the crisis in service provision which CAFCASS has experienced, and the establishment of a body which is able successfully to coordinate and extend support services for families experiencing relationship breakdown, requires firm leadership and clear decision-making structures. Neither have been apparent in CAFCASS so far, and both are significantly more difficult to achieve in the context of the confused relationship we have described.

The CAFCASS Board

120. These and other problems might have been avoided had CAFCASS had a strong Board, with responsive Chairmanship, which understood its role and was prepared to offer the leadership and strategic guidance which was necessary for the task of setting up a new organisation. There was a widespread feeling amongst our witnesses that this has not been the case.[203]

121. Problems with the Board began with the failure to ensure its timely establishment, as detailed above.[204] Even once it was established, however, serious doubts emerged about the range of experience and expertise represented on it. Peter Harris, the former Official Solicitor, once again sums up the feeling amongst witnesses when he says,

> The Board of CAFCASS consists of a Chair and 10 members. The Chairman was formerly the Chairman of Scope and latterly has been a management consultant. Of the other ten members only one, Leonie Jordan, a practising solicitor, has any direct experience of children proceedings or court reporting. While several other board members have experience of social services, none appears to have experience of involvement in child care proceedings or advising the courts. The only other Board Member to have had experience in these matters resigned from the Board within 7 months of appointment.

He concludes, "It seems regrettable that the body with the statutory duty of providing children's guardians and children and family reporters, to safeguard the interests of children in litigation and to provide advice to the courts, should have so little knowledge of the nature of the business in respect of which it is responsible."[205] Kit Chivers, Chief Inspector of Court Services, reflected that view when he said, in the foreword to his Unit's most recent Report on CAFCASS, that the Service "needs people of recognised stature on its side to help shape the strategic choices and to lend them authority."[206]

122. A late submission from an individual Board member confirmed our concerns about the ineffective operation of the Board during the difficult early period. Whilst she notes some recent improvements, particularly following the appointment of the current Chief Executive, she suggests that the Board remains "disempowered and unable to make a

---

[202] Ev 215–216, Q 200
[203] Ev 87 para 12, 95 para 3, 113 para 19, 146 para 8.2, 161 para 1.20, 170 para 8.10, 181 para 14, 197 s 2, 214–216, 226–230, 249–250; Qq 6, 167 [Mr Griffith-Jones], 201, 204, etc
[204] Para 27 ff
[205] Ev 113 para 19
[206] *Setting a Course*, op cit, Chief Inspector's Foreword

valued contribution to the oversight and strategic direction of CAFCASS."[207] Two particular points in that memorandum reflect concerns we have raised.

123. Firstly, **it is clear that the confused lines of accountability between LCD, CAFCASS and the Senior Management Team, particularly the Chief Executive, are seriously hampering the Board's ability to make an effective contribution.**[208] As we say above, we can understand the desire of Ministers to keep a close eye on the Service. It is quite proper for the relevant Minister to meet the Board Chairman on a regular basis and to monitor the operation of the Service. When the Board is bypassed by the direct involvement of the Chief Executive and senior LCD officials, it is left disempowered and unable to fulfil its role effectively. Secondly, **the lack of relevant experience and expertise on the Board make it important that it is not reliant solely on the senior management team for information about the service**. Our witness's complaint that Board members do not yet have access to the CAFCASS Intranet and "are discouraged from receiving information about the work of CAFCASS other than from management"[209] is therefore a matter for considerable concern.

124. Clearly the Board was hampered by the appointment of the first Chief Executive, who turned out to be so unsuitable for the job that she was eventually dismissed. Even taking this into account, however, **there is no doubt that it has failed to deal effectively with the task with which it is entrusted.** The most obvious example of this was the Board decision, early in its existence, to withdraw the offer of self-employment—the decision which was overturned at judicial review. Since then, the Board has failed to re-establish confidence in its ability to provide strategic direction and effectively hold the senior management team to account. **The Board has not given the impression that it has any clear idea of how CAFCASS should be re-establishing itself as an effective organisation.**

---

[207] Ev 226–228
[208] Ev 229 para 6.2, 249 para 3.2
[209] Ev 229 para 6.3

7 The way forward

125. The situation we have described above, from the evidence we have received, is not a happy one. It shows an organisation which is respected neither by all its own staff nor by many of its partners and stakeholders; which is failing to provide its core services in a timely and effective manner; and which has been unable to make any progress in fulfilling the hopes expressed for it in providing new and coordinated support services for children and families experiencing relationship breakdown.

126. It is only fair to say, though, that this picture does not fully do justice to the good work which has been done both by individual practitioners and, to some extent, by senior management since the Service was established. Even following the bleakest period in CAFCASS's history, in the months after set-up, MCSI was able to report that "front-line services [had] to a very large extent been maintained."[210] In his Foreword to MCSI's latest report, the Chief Inspector says, "the storm has abated and patches of blue sky are beginning to appear… A strategy is now emerging which will lead… to a more effective, better managed service in future years."[211] Those of us who have visited individual CAFCASS regions have seen that view reflected in the attitude of staff and management who are now gaining confidence in the ability of the organisation to set itself properly on its feet. The recently-published Corporate Plan, too, gives some grounds for optimism in the signs of ambition which CAFCASS is beginning to show. In many ways, therefore, the views which have been expressed by our witnesses reflect the CAFCASS of a year ago, rather than the CAFCASS of today.

127. Nonetheless, on the basis of the evidence we have received and which we set out above, we retain significant concerns about CAFCASS's ability to perform its core tasks and develop its services in the way we believe Parliament intended. In this chapter, we discuss the response of the organisation and of the Department to the concerns which have been raised, and set out our view of what needs to be done to set CAFCASS on the right course.

Failures in service provision

128. Of most urgent concern is the issue of delay in the allocation of cases to guardians in public law and in the completion of reports in private law. The principle of "no delay" is fundamental to the legislative framework within which CAFCASS works and to ensuring that children get the service they need. CAFCASS successfully defended itself against the judicial review case in which it was argued that CAFCASS was under a legal duty to appoint a children's guardian immediately. Nevertheless the organisation recognised, and it was affirmed by the court, that "the sooner that an officer of the service is made available for appointment and starts work as the children's guardian, the better it is for that child, his family and… the court that has to make decisions about the upbringing of that child."[212] Until these decisions are made, the child may be a position of bewildering uncertainty and

---

[210] *Setting Up*, Chief Inspector's Foreword
[211] *Setting a Course*, Chief Inspector's Foreword
[212] R v CAFCASS [2003] EWHC Admin 235, para 95

isolation from family members and friends. It is vital that both in public and in private law delay is kept to a minimum.

129. We were concerned, therefore, at suggestions that delay was, despite CAFCASS's comments in the judicial review, being "institutionalised" within CAFCASS. The comments attributed to the Chief Executive in the interview mentioned above[213] prompted fears that CAFCASS would simply accept a situation in which vulnerable children are expected just to wait for as long as it takes for a guardian to become available.[214] CAFCASS's Corporate Plan did little to allay those fears, setting as it did a target in public law of 80% allocation within 7 days.[215] Whilst a considerable improvement on the current situation, such a target represented a failure even to aspire to the standards attained pre-CAFCASS, where allocation within 24 hours was typical.[216]

130. **We were pleased, therefore, to hear the Chief Executive affirm CAFCASS's intention to aim for allocation of guardians within 48 hours.**[217] This intention has subsequently been recognised in the judicial case management protocol for care cases recently agreed by the Advisory Committee on Judicial Case Management.[218] **We hope that this target can be speedily achieved. It should be formally recognised in CAFCASS's performance targets.**

131. Whilst apparently less demanding than the typical time for allocation pre-CAFCASS, we acknowledge the sense in most cases in leaving a little more time so as to ensure that not just the next available guardian, but the most suitable guardian available, can be allocated to a case. However, in certain types of cases—for example, applications for emergency protection or secure accommodation orders—cases can be heard at less than 24 hours' notice. Such cases potentially involve the separation of parent and child, or locking up a child without criminal proceedings, and affect over 2500 children every year. It is therefore vital that guardians are available for the speediest possible allocation to these cases.[219] **We recommend that CAFCASS set a separate target—which should be as close to 100% as it is reasonably possible to get—for the allocation of a guardian in time for the first hearing in these cases.**

132. In private law, the Corporate Plan target is that at least 95% of requests in the month be allocated 10 weeks before the filing date, in order to ensure that adequate time is allowed for preparation of the report so that it can be available for the next hearing.[220] Here at least CAFCASS does not appear to be accepting standards any lower than those which were achieved pre-CAFCASS. There is nevertheless still a serious problem with delay in private law cases. CAFCASS cannot address this problem unilaterally, but it is a key part of the system. **CAFCASS should play a full part in improving the service given to children and**

---

[213] Para 110
[214] Ev 244 paras 4–5 and 7
[215] *op cit*, p 24
[216] See para 61 and note
[217] Q 262
[218] *New protocol to reduce delay in care cases*, Department for Constitutional Affairs Press Notice, 18 June 2003
[219] Ev 249 para 4.5
[220] *op cit*, p 24

families in the family courts, by improving its own performance and by contributing to joint efforts to reduce delay across the system.

CAFCASS Legal

133. We are also concerned by the evidence we have heard of the reduction in the service provided by CAFCASS Legal. It is deeply regrettable that it should have found itself unable to take on cases which the Official Solicitor would previously have expected to deal with. **It is important that the shortage of staff in CAFCASS Legal is not forgotten as CAFCASS deals with the difficulties it is experiencing elsewhere in the service. We recommend that such resources be made available to CAFCASS Legal as to enable it at least to match the service provided before it by the Official Solicitor.**

Dealing with the backlog

134. There are some welcome signs that CAFCASS is beginning to get to grips with its service delivery duties. We were told that, in terms of its present caseload, CAFCASS is now broadly matching guardian allocation to case inflow.[221] There remains, however, the problem of the backlog which has built up in the two years since CAFCASS was established. In a supplementary memorandum to our inquiry, CAFCASS sets out the measures which it has taken to increase capacity and deal with the backlog.[222] **These are all welcome, though there is little sign as yet that they have made a significant impact on the backlog of cases.**[223] **We hope that the judicial case management protocol referred to above, to which CAFCASS has signed up, will decrease delay in care cases.**[224] **The only way in which CAFCASS is truly going to get on top of its service delivery duties is by dealing with its staff shortage.**[225] We deal with this issue below.

Recruitment and workforce planning

135. We recognise that CAFCASS is working in a difficult context where recruitment is concerned. Experienced and even newly qualified social work professionals are very much at a premium, as recent surveys of local authority social services departments have found.[226] A concerted effort will therefore be needed to attract the staff required to achieve the targets set out above.

136. The question which needs to be answered first of all, however, is what level of staff resources are going to be needed in order to ensure that an appropriate level of service can be provided. CAFCASS's supplementary memorandum records that "the budget provides for the whole time equivalent of a further 132 practitioners".[227] There is no indication, however, of whether those additional practitioners will bring CAFCASS up to a situation where it is able to clear the backlog; or even to cope with the current level of demand.

---

[221] Ev 231; Q 256
[222] Ev 236
[223] See para 62 above
[224] See para 130
[225] Ev 231
[226] Ev 235 para 2.2; Q 104
[227] Ev 237 para 5.1

Indeed, there is no indication that CAFCASS even knows what level of staffing it needs to be able to cope with demand, or what combination of employed and self-employed guardians will best enable the organisation to cope with the fluctuations in what is predominantly a demand-led service.[228]

137. This is particularly important in the context of a likely increase in demand for CAFCASS's services. The number of care cases has been rising steadily over recent years, and there is no indication that that trend is likely to decrease. Commencement of the provisions of section 122 of the Adoption and Children Act may increase demand still further.[229, 230] We also heard evidence that the age profile of CAFCASS's current workforce is increasing, with a large number of staff possibly approaching retirement age.[231] This too will add to the problems CAFCASS faces with recruitment.

138. This brings us to the issue of workforce planning. CAFCASS has to be able to live within the budget it has been allocated by the LCD. However, it also needs to be in a position where it knows what it can and cannot achieve within that budget. If CAFCASS cannot achieve the standards expected of it within the budget it has been allowed, it must either take that case to Ministers and request further resources; or be quite clear that it has to find new ways of fulfilling its duties. This goes wider than simply recruitment and staff resources; but it is in this area that the issue is most obvious and most urgent.

139. **We recommend that CAFCASS urgently undertake comprehensive workforce planning, in order to identify accurately current and future staffing requirements.** This exercise should include:

- an assessment of the staff resources required

    - to allocate and follow up all public law cases without unreasonable delay and carry out all investigations needed in the best interests of the children concerned; and

    - to allocate all private law cases within a reasonable timescale and to give sufficient time to each case to ensure than the best interests of the children can be properly presented to the court

    taking into account anticipated increases in demand;

- an assessment of likely future recruitment needs given the age profile of the current workforce; and

- an assessment of the combination of employed and self-employed staff which will best enable CAFCASS to cope with fluctuations in demand for its services.

---

[228] Ev 199, 239, 244 para 8
[229] See para 52 above
[230] Qq 101, 129
[231] Ev 178 para 15

Attracting back experienced guardians

140. In the meantime, one particular group which could be used to help CAFCASS out of its current difficulties are the self-employed guardians who have left the service. Opinion amongst witnesses was divided as to the extent to which it would be possible for CAFCASS to attract such people back. Arran Poyser of MCSI suggested that, for some, one simply had to accept that they were not coming back, and move on.[232] Others, though, stressed the contribution which such people could make, noted how important it was that efforts be made to attract at least some of them back to the Service, and suggested that it would be possible to do so.[233] Given their experience, these staff could prove invaluable in making a rapid impact on the current backlog. New recruits naturally take some time to come up to speed, as the Chief Executive pointed out to us in evidence.[234] Recognising the progress which CAFCASS has already made in improving terms and conditions for guardians,[235] **we recommend that CAFCASS take further steps to target recruitment on experienced guardians.** We acknowledge that the success of any such steps will depend on significant progress being made in addressing some of the reasons why guardians left the service in the first place.[236]

Longer-term recruitment

141. In the longer term, CAFCASS could help itself by joining the current drive to attract and to retain more talented people into the social work professions. The Association of Directors of Social Services recommended that "CAFCASS should consider working with ADSS and the Department of Health[237] on a workforce strategy to contribute to the development of a pool of highly skilled children's social workers from which Children's Guardians can be drawn."[238] **We recommend that CAFCASS follow up this suggestion.**

Standard of work done by new recruits

142. Concerns expressed by some witnesses about the standard of work done by some new recruits are worrying. However, we have been assured both by the Chief Executive and by representatives of CAFCASS front-line managers that there has been no diminution in the quality of the people concerned.[239] The issue appears to us to be one of the lack of appropriate training: to which we turn now.

Training and professional development

143. CAFCASS's failure to establish even a minimum training and professional development strand appears to us to be one of the more serious of CAFCASS's early

---

[232] Q 11. See also Q 228 [Ms Doughty]
[233] Ev 248 para 5(ii); Qq 93, 121, 156, 228 [Mr Barnes], 229
[234] Q 266
[235] Ev 236 para 4.1
[236] Q 152 ff
[237] Responsibility for Government policy on recruitment of social workers is now shared with the Department for Education and Skills, following the appointment of a Minister for Children based in that Department [see footnote 1 above].
[238] Ev 220 para 6. See also Q 147
[239] Ev 239; Q 266

period. It is only through training that the very foundations of practice and the principles that underpin that practice can be clarified. Training is a vitally important part of the development of any professional; but is particularly important for those dealing with children, where actions taken now can have a profound effect on their development. Training can help to challenge the often held assumptions that adults necessarily know better than children, which can lead to misinterpretation of children's statements to accord with adult views; and paternalistic approaches which undermine children's capacity to engage with and contribute to decisions about their own lives. The interface of families and social services departments with the courts is a complex area for which initial professional training in social work alone does not equip social workers.

144. The failure to establish such a strand is all the more culpable because of the ready availability of material on which to base its establishment. As we note above, systems for self-help and professional development were already running before CAFCASS.[240] There also existed a number of known and respected training courses put together by NAGALRO, the professional association for children's guardians, and others.[241] Some progress—though it is impossible to tell how much—was made in this area by the relevant working group of the Project Team. Like so much else of the Project Team's work, it was simply not used.[242]

Induction training

145. Worst of all, in our view, is the failure to provide proper induction training for new recruits. What witnesses described to us as no more than a "trip around the bay"[243] cannot do justice to a highly skilled and important professional role. The evidence suggests that the consequent ill-preparedness of recruits has been demonstrated on a number of occasions through the reports which lawyers and the courts have seen.[244] **It would be unacceptable for new recruits to continue to be allowed to undertake this important work without the benefit of a proper course of training. The task of ascertaining and communicating to the court the child's wishes and feelings, as part of the process of determining what is in the child's best interests, should be central to that training.**[245]

Convergence

146. We appreciate the potential benefits to be gained from the convergence of the roles of children's guardians and court welfare officers. We are, however, concerned that such moves as are being taken towards achieving this aim should not be done in the absence of a proper appreciation by senior management of the differences between the two roles. We were to some extent reassured by the comments of the Chief Executive when we questioned him on this matter,[246] but as we note elsewhere doubts still remain over the

---

[240] Para 70
[241] Qq 163, 208
[242] Ev 130; Qq 208, 232
[243] Ev 129
[244] Para 68
[245] Q 29
[246] Q 275

quality of the training which is to be provided to allow convergence to take place. **Convergence in the work of practitioners from the two different strands needs to be handled with respect for the different skills and knowledge people bring.** In particular, **convergence cannot be carried forward in the absence of properly developed training and development programmes which give the necessary preparation and backup for those moving into new areas of work**, especially concerning their role in relation to children. Convergence will necessarily require practitioners to maintain knowledge in two different and not necessarily convergent areas of practice.

Performance management

147. **CAFCASS must also face the issue of performance management.** Not only is the provision of professional support and development vital for an organisation which relies so heavily on its front-line practitioners, but it is essential that appropriate standards should be set by management and met by staff, including self-employed practitioners and agency workers. Only if such standards are set and met can it be ensured that all CAFCASS's clients are receiving an appropriate level of service.

148. **In setting standards CAFCASS should seek to draw on the expertise of its existing workforce, and the bodies which represent them. It should involve the Board and organisations which represent parents or children and commission and make use of research.** This will all take time, but this is not a reason to delay the introduction of some aspects of performance management—for example, the introduction of regular review sessions with line managers for front-line practitioners—as a first step to securing and developing practice standards across the piece.

149. **Local managers will need training and support to carry out this function.** The use of external consultants who assisted with appraisal in the pre-CAFCASS days may be desirable, particularly where managers have only limited knowledge or experience of the work undertaken by front-line staff. Local managers would also be considerably assisted in this role by the introduction of an electronic case management system, a matter which we discuss further below.[247] The introduction of such a system would not only free up local managers' time currently expended on routine collection of information, but would also allow robust comparisons to be made between, for example, the amount of time spent on various types of cases.

Progress in the provision of training

150. Only now are substantive efforts being made to address the lacunae in the provision of training, and to ensure that training is afforded proper priority in the organisation's planning.[248] We are pleased to hear of the announcement of the letting of a training contract with Royal Holloway College. Doubts remained, however, at the time of our inquiry, about what exactly the courses which would be provided would entail, and how they would be quality assured.[249] More importantly, there is still little sign that CAFCASS is

---

[247] Para 154 ff
[248] Q 29 ff
[249] Qq 29, 163

prepared to give training and development the profile and resources within the organisation which it needs.

151. **CAFCASS must ensure that all four aspects of the training agenda—induction and substantive training for new recruits; induction training for experienced social workers who need introducing and orientating to CAFCASS; in-service training and professional development; and convergence training—are addressed by the establishment of a dedicated training and development strand within CAFCASS.** This strand should have high-level representation within the senior management team and appropriate external involvement. **We recommend that an individual Board member or sub-group with appropriate experience or expertise should oversee its development and ongoing work.** The role of this member or sub-group will not be to micro-manage the work of the unit, nor to dictate the content of the training and development provided. The member or sub-group should, however, ensure that the unit is established in a timely manner, and that the appropriate quality assurance systems are in place.

Information Technology

152. **There is an urgent need for an integrated case management system for CAFCASS.** The failure of senior management to recognise and effectively address this need in the two years since the original project was halted is hugely regrettable. We are particularly concerned by the claims of the CAFCASS Managers Association of a lack of consultation with users about their needs, which seems to us to lie at the root of CAFCASS's failures in this area.[250] We are also concerned by the rickety nature of the systems which are currently being used to collect information about service needs and the conduct of cases.[251]

153. The Chief Executive told us that moves were now being made to establish what he described as a "case recording system", with the aim of establishing proper support for the collection of management information.[252] The answer to a written Parliamentary Question on IT systems for CAFCASS gives further details of the planned introduction of the system.[253] However, neither the Chief Executive's comments nor the written answer indicate that there has been the full user involvement from the start of the project which will be necessary if the new system is to meet their needs. We doubt whether the "simpler" system which is planned will be adequate in the medium term to meet all the requirements of a modern service. The promise of "incremental development" may have prudence in its favour, but is likely to be inadequate to ensure the speedy establishment of a much-needed comprehensive system.[254]

154. Until a properly functioning case management system is in place,

- it will be impossible to have full confidence in the reliability of the data on which plans for those resource needs are based[255]

---

[250] Ev 239, 240; Q 234. See also Ev 155 para 11(b)
[251] Q 241 ff
[252] Q 282
[253] HC Deb (30 June 2003) col 128W
[254] Ev 234 para 1.2
[255] Q 283

- data for the research which is urgently needed into the conduct and outcome of CAFCASS's work will be much more difficult to obtain

- front-line managers and administrative staff in CAFCASS will continue to labour under unnecessarily high workloads

- the security, and thus confidentiality, of existing records cannot be guaranteed.

155. We recognise that CAFCASS needs to beware of falling foul of the problems which have beset public sector IT projects. That history, however, does not in any way lessen the urgent need for the establishment of an appropriate system. **We recommend that CAFCASS re-establish a project board and give it the task of setting out a clear timetable for the establishment of a fully fledged case management system.** There should be wide consultation with users both within and, where appropriate, outside CAFCASS on the shape of the system, and there should be user representation on the project board throughout. As with training, above, **an individual Board member or sub-group should oversee (not micro-manage) the project.** Whilst the timetable for the establishment of such a system should be realistic, both in budgetary and project management terms, budgetary constraints should not be allowed to get in the way of its establishment. **The new Department may need to make additional resources available to secure this crucial aspect of CAFCASS's proper functioning to ensure the timely establishment of an appropriate system.**

Support services

156. Whilst areas such as training, IT and the delivery of core services have been the biggest failures of CAFCASS's early period, support services have been the biggest disappointment to those who welcomed the establishment of a unified service. The concentration on the problems of setup has left CAFCASS unable to deliver on the wider agenda which had been promised. Regrettably, we share the conclusion of many of our witnesses and indeed of CAFCASS itself that this situation must continue to prevail for the time being.[256] **Until the delivery of core services is secure, CAFCASS cannot risk diverting significant resources into developing support services.**

Need to indicate role in provision of support services

157. With signs that CAFCASS may finally be getting to grips with the delivery of its core services, however, comes renewed hope that it might be able at least to start showing the way forward for support services. The Chief Executive[257] and the Minister[258] drew attention to a number of initiatives which CAFCASS has taken in this field; and these are encouraging. There is, however, no sense that those efforts add up to a coherent programme for the development of support services by CAFCASS.[259] **There is a feeling amongst voluntary organisations working in this field that CAFCASS's failure to give**

---

[256] Ev 97 s 2, 208, 239; Qq 108 and 214
[257] Q 290
[258] Q 317
[259] Ev 242 para 1.11

clear indication of the way it might look to develop this aspect of its remit is hindering the development of services by others. **CAFCASS needs to make clear what long-term role it envisages for itself in the provision of support services for children and families experiencing relationship breakdown.**

158. Our view is that the services which should be provided to children and families experiencing relationship breakdown should be integrated with the full range of services available to children in a wide variety of other settings. We also consider that CAFCASS needs to focus its own efforts above all on its core task of securing the welfare of children in court proceedings through representation and reporting. These considerations suggest to us that CAFCASS can most appropriately play a coordinating role in ensuring that the proper provision is available for the children with which it works, rather than attempting to provide the services itself. **We recommend that the Minister for Children consult with CAFCASS and other interested parties about a proposal that the organisation should take a strategic/co-ordinating/funding role for support services rather than providing them itself.**

159. Progress on this issue may also help in other ways. As Judith Timms of NYAS says,

> a clear declaration of intent and a commitment to proactive principles of prevention and support could set a clear agenda for the development of the service which could inform current debates about management structures and set a path towards an integrated service which is both effective in safeguarding children and cost-effective in providing best value for money.[260]

Funding for support services

160. The inherent problems of setting up a new organisation and difficulties in the provision of core services are not, however, the only reason why progress in the development of support services has been slow. CAFCASS has suffered significant budget constraints in its early period. Indications are that recent increases have now brought CAFCASS close to a level where it has sufficient funds to meet its core responsibilities (although even this is not certain, hence our recommendation above regarding the conduct of a detailed workforce planning exercise[261]). **If CAFCASS is to make a significant long-term contribution to the development of support services, however, we expect the Department will need to increase funding further.**[262] Any such investment would not be wasted. As *Making Contact Work* recognised,

> a properly functioning expanded CAFCASS will result in substantial savings in other areas of the system—fewer contested court proceedings, with consequential substantial savings in both time and money spent in court, without counting the more intangible emotional benefits to children and families brought about by the amicable resolution of contact disputes.[263]

---

[260] Ev 146 para 8.1
[261] Para 139
[262] Ev 126
[263] *op cit*, Letter to the Lord Chancellor. See also Ev 178 para 14

Cooperation with other bodies

161. Witnesses were keen to emphasise that CAFCASS is not working in a vacuum where support services are concerned.[264] **The development of its role in the provision of such services requires close consultation and cooperation with all other bodies, statutory and voluntary, working in this field.**

162. **CAFCASS needs to work much more closely than appears to have been the case hitherto with the Legal Services Commission (LSC).** At the time of publication of this Report, the continued role of the LSC in projects such as FAInS is uncertain (following the transfer of family and parenting law and support to DfES under the Minister for Children). We hope that any transfer of responsibilities which does take place will offer the opportunity to involve CAFCASS much more closely in this initiative. Whatever happens to those responsibilities, however, CAFCASS will need to retain—or, in the light of the evidence we have seen, develop—close links with the LSC. Notwithstanding the machinery of government changes, the LSC will continue to play an important role in public funding for court proceedings, including necessary expert assessments and support services aimed at reducing disputes or diverting families from the courts. It is therefore vital that the two bodies work closely together.

163. **We hope that close working will enable value for money to be achieved in the provision of appropriate services whilst avoiding the narrow self-interest apparent so far in relations between the two bodies.**[265] In the case of public law proceedings, the entire cost falls on the public purse. Joined-up government demands high levels of co-operation between the various central and local government departments, agencies and NDPBs. Anything less not only risks wasting scarce resources, but would be a betrayal of the children whose very well-being depends on the quality and timeliness of all aspects of the system.

164. **CAFCASS must work together closely with others in the family justice and child protection system.** We were very greatly concerned by reports of withdrawal of CAFCASS team managers from liaison arrangements with the courts and local authorities.[266] **The Minister for Children and the CAFCASS Board should urgently review the claim by the CAFCASS Managers Association that many front line managers are having to withdraw from liaison arrangements. CAFCASS should take steps to ensure that there is full co-operation at all times.**

165. The good links CAFCASS has already established with the judiciary will stand it in good stead when it transfers to the Department for Education and Skills. Meanwhile, that transfer and **the collection of children's services within that Department provides an opportunity for CAFCASS to renew its links with other organisations working with children, and ensure that the joined-up working demanded by the Victoria Climbié case, and others before it, is achieved.**

---

[264] Q 215
[265] Para 88 ff
[266] Ev 239; Q 220

Research and improving practice

166. It is also very disappointing that the new service has not resulted in the expansion of research capacity. **There is, as MCSI has identified, a significant gap in knowledge about "what works" in family proceedings related work which CAFCASS needs to fill.** In particular, only when that gap is filled can CAFCASS begin to address in a credible manner some of the complaints raised in evidence to us by non-resident parents and those concerned with domestic violence issues. More broadly, **it is vital for the sake of all the children with whom CAFCASS is concerned that it discovers what works for children experiencing family breakdown, establishes how its practitioners can best contribute to the well-being of children involved in court proceedings or their aftermath, and ensures that best practice is developed accordingly. The establishment of a practice development unit, which CAFCASS intends to have in place by December this year, is a step in the right direction.**[267] **Significant further progress in the development of research capacity will, however, be needed if CAFCASS is to achieve those aims.**

167. One way of beginning to find out "what works" would be to ask experienced practitioners and former practitioners. Such an exercise could only take place in the context of properly commissioned and conducted research, but could be one way of re-engaging CAFCASS with people whose skills it has lost.

Management and organisational culture

168. There are signs that CAFCASS has not taken seriously the concerns which have been expressed about its management practices and organisational culture. The organisation has faced very significant difficulties in its early period, not all of which have been of its own making. Nevertheless it appears to us that CAFCASS has to some extent been using those difficulties which have not been of its own making—harmonisation of all the terms and conditions of employment which it inherited from predecessor organisations, for example, or the concerns of the Inland Revenue about the terms of the self-employed contract—as cover for bad decisions and inappropriate prioritising of its own. Problems in the allocation of cases, for example, cannot in our view be put down to increases in demand[268] or the shortage of experienced social workers alone, significant though those problems are.[269] Rather, the perceived emphasis on management over quality of service, and the alienation of a section of its workforce—to the point where one experienced guardian can say of CAFCASS that "it is now not an organisation that the best quality professionals want to align themselves with"[270]—have led to a situation where many suitably qualified people simply do not want to work for the organisation, and left CAFCASS struggling to find practitioners capable of effectively fulfilling its key duties.

169. The appointment of a new Chief Executive—albeit that he has not yet been permanently appointed—appears to have resulted in a significant improvement in the running of the organisation, and witnesses have recognised that improvement.[271] But the

---

[267] Ev 237–238
[268] Q 256 ff
[269] Ev 240
[270] Q 152
[271] Ev 155 para 11(c), 228 s 6.1

legacy of those early months is still with the organisation, and it is still taking decisions—such as that to introduce an additional tier of management—which tend to give the impression that it is more interested in its own organisational structures than in delivering the best possible service for children.[272]

170. **It is important that this Report is not seen merely as an endorsement of the criticisms which have been made about CAFCASS. It is vital that CAFCASS work together with the professional and voluntary organisations who have expressed their concerns to us to address the issues which have been raised in this Report, and it is equally vital that the organisations concerned recognise that, in the interests of the children they serve, a positive climate now needs to be created. CAFCASS needs to be helped to use, develop and build on the considerable skills which exist among its personnel and to become the kind of quality organisation it was originally intended to be.**

171. **Nevertheless, if it is to regain the confidence of all those who work with and for it, CAFCASS needs to demonstrate clearly and unambiguously that it is putting children and young people first in all that it does.** This will not necessarily be easy to achieve, and it may take some time; but the sooner progress is made, the sooner CAFCASS will be able to become, as the Chief Inspector of MCSI said it should become, "an organisation which all its staff are proud to work for and which is recognised by the professional community as the national centre of expertise in its field."[273]

172. **We recommend that the CAFCASS Board identify three or four key actions which it can take which will demonstrate that it is truly "putting children and young people first".** These actions should not represent "business as usual", but should be designed to show that the problems of the early times are behind it and that the organisation is ready to assume a different and more appropriate focus on the children it serves. **Such a refocusing of priorities should work through into a longer-term position where CAFCASS judges all that it does against the question "Will this improve the service we offer to children and the courts?"**

173. We do not wish CAFCASS to continue to be seen to be prioritising management issues at the expense of delivery of front-line services. However, one way in which the Service could demonstrate that it is taking concerns about management style seriously would be to examine how it could implement the "bottom-up creative approach" referred to in the submission we received from a Board member. In evidence to us, the CAFCASS Chairman assured us that he "really [did] want to see" what a "light management touch" meant in practice, on the ground.[274] **We recommend that, rather than waiting to be shown how such an approach might work, the CAFCASS Board establish a working group to discuss both with its own stakeholders and with others with relevant expertise outside the organisation how such an approach could be implemented.** In particular, this group could learn from other organisations which have adopted a similar approach.

---

[272] Ev 245 para 18
[273] *Setting a Course*, Chief Inspector's Foreword
[274] Q 269

The Framework Document and CAFCASS's relationship with government

174. The history of CAFCASS's relationship with government has not been a happy one. Blurred lines of accountability, poor funding decisions and a failure on the part of both the Department and the Board to understand the proper constitutional relationship between an NDPB and its parent Department were significant hindrances to the successful resolution of the problems which have beset CAFCASS—and, in some cases, were significant factors in the creation of those problems. **The transfer of responsibility for CAFCASS away from the Lord Chancellor's Department, as was, to the Department for Education and Skills offers an opportunity for a reassessment and recasting of the relationship between CAFCASS and its parent Department.** The relocation can be seen as a welcome recognition that CAFCASS is primarily a service for children. We hope that reporting to the Minister for Children will cause CAFCASS to reassess its priorities.

175. In particular, there is now an opportunity to redraft the Framework Document in a manner which is more appropriate for an NDPB and which more closely reflects CAFCASS's core duties. The Framework Document is, primarily, a description of the relationship between the organisation and Government, but it should also clearly reflect the organisation's core tasks. **We recommend that, when the Framework Document is redrafted to take account of the new Departmental responsibilities, the DfES ensure that the new document both explicitly reflects CAFCASS's core task of securing the welfare of children in court proceedings through representation and reporting, and sets out the proper constitutional relationship between CAFCASS as an NDPB and its parent Department.** Furthermore, **whilst CAFCASS remains an NDPB**—and, notwithstanding the views of MCSI, we are not convinced of the need for any change to its status—**its parent Department must ensure that it is able to function as such and must respect the independence from Government which comes with that status.**

176. Whilst the transfer to the Department for Education and Skills will provide an opportunity to recast the relationship between CAFCASS and its parent Department, it also poses some risks. This Department has no history of involvement in the work which CAFCASS does, and the only relevant knowledge base within it will be that provided by any civil servants who transfer over from the LCD at the same time. CAFCASS itself must take responsibility for securing the improvements in service delivery which we have identified as essential to its establishment as an effective organisation. In doing so, however, it will need the support and, where appropriate, advice of its parent Department. There is some evidence that when CAFCASS was originally established within the Lord Chancellor's Department, and the services it provided moved away from the Home Office and Department of Health, there was a failure in knowledge transfer which contributed to the loss of focus on CAFCASS's core role. It would be deeply regrettable if the transfer of CAFCASS to the purview of another Department were now to lead to a further loss of knowledge and expertise amongst those who should be supporting the Service.

The CAFCASS Board

177. Thus far, the Board has failed to provide the necessary strategic direction and accountability which CAFCASS so desperately needs. Nor has it operated in an effective

manner which has allowed the concerns of individual Board members and stakeholders to be discussed and addressed.[275]

178. Part of the blame for the failure of the Board to perform its duties effectively must also lie with Ministers. The Board is demonstrably short of expertise in a number of key areas, including the specific work of CAFCASS practitioners, setting up new organisations, running NDPBs, and the governance of national service delivery and policy developing organisations.[276] Although both the Minister[277] and the CAFCASS Chairman[278] attempted to deny that the Board was short of such expertise, we were unconvinced by their arguments. We do not consider that having a son or daughter working in the family court system is a substitute for relevant expertise on the part of a Board member.[279] The failure to appoint more members with greater experience and expertise has been a significant hindrance to the Board's effective operation. It has also lent further weight to the suspicions that the LCD wished to exercise greater control over the organisation than was appropriate for an NDPB: the fact that the Minister boasts of not just one or two but several Board members having experience as management consultants tells its own story.[280]

179. Unless significant improvements are made soon, confidence in the ability of the Board to perform its duties effectively will wane further. Recent signs are not encouraging. The Board's response to the submission sent to us by one of its members is deeply depressing.[281] The Chairman and other Board members seem determined to bury their heads in the sand and pretend there is nothing wrong, rather than taking the steps necessary to assert the position of the Board as an effective driver for improvement.

180. The transfer of responsibility for the appointment of members of the Board from the Lord Chancellor to the Minister for Children and the recasting of the Framework Document present an opportunity to re-examine the experience and expertise present on the Board. **It is a central recommendation of this Report that there should be a fundamental review of membership of the Board. We believe the Board needs people of experience and stature who can develop the strategy necessary to deliver an effective, child-centred service.**

181. **The new Board must take steps to ensure that it is able to carry out effectively its function of providing strategic direction and holding senior management to account.** It must not allow itself to be as dependent on senior management as the current Board, nor to be bypassed in discussions with the Department. We hope that the tasks we have proposed for the Board in overseeing the implementation of certain key recommendations will be a start in enabling it to work effectively. In the longer term, it is for every Board member to consider how they, individually and collectively, can best contribute to the effective running of the organisation.

---

[275] Ev 227–229
[276] Ev 226 para 1.2
[277] Ev 230–231
[278] Q 289
[279] *ibid*
[280] Ev 231
[281] Ev 238

Inspection regime

182. The change in Departmental arrangements came too late for us to take any evidence on the implications of CAFCASS's transfer to the Department for Education and Skills for the inspection regime to which the service is subject. It appears to us nevertheless that, as a social work organisation as well as a service for the courts, CAFCASS should come under the rigorous and independent scrutiny of a social care inspectorate. Such arrangements would help to reinforce CAFCASS's focus on the children which it serves. In order to recognise both sides of CAFCASS's work, and to preserve continuity in senior personnel undertaking inspections, **we recommend that joint inspection arrangements be established between the new Commission for Social Care Inspection (CSCI) and the CAFCASS Inspection Unit of HM Magistrates' Court Services Inspectorate (MCSI).**

Continued Parliamentary scrutiny of CAFCASS's work

183. With the transfer of responsibility for CAFCASS away from the Lord Chancellor's Department and into the Department for Education and Skills passes also responsibility for the Parliamentary scrutiny of CAFCASS away from this Committee to the Education and Skills Committee. That Committee will of course determine its own priorities. **We hope nonetheless that there will continue to be active Parliamentary oversight of CAFCASS's important work, and of the progress being made in addressing the recommendations we make in this Report. The children CAFCASS serves deserve no less.**

Conclusions and recommendations

Acknowledging the devotion of CAFCASS practitioners

1. We wish to acknowledge the skill and devotion of staff throughout the organisation and their commitment to the children they serve. The criticisms we make of the way CAFCASS's difficulties have been handled should not detract from that fact. (Paragraph 5)

Effect of the short timetable

2. The decision to proceed on [a foreshortened] timetable was a serious misjudgement. The Government should not have allowed the timetable for the establishment of the National Probation Service to dictate the unrealistic programme for the establishment of CAFCASS. The decision to do so makes CAFCASS appear of secondary importance. The impression was gained that the Departmental priorities of the Lord Chancellor's Department were secondary to those of the Home Office. It is vital that all Government Ministers give priority to work with children in line with their commitments under the UN Convention on the Rights of the Child (Paragraph 26)

Appointment of the Board and senior management team

3. Contingency plans should, however, have been in place to deal with [the foreshortened timetable]. In particular, it is difficult to understand why a shadow Board was not set up, with an indication that permanent appointment was subject to the passage of the Bill. (Paragraph 29)

Establishment of the service: conclusion

4. The overall impression gained from consideration of the circumstances leading up to the establishment of CAFCASS is that even prior to its establishment there was a lack of high-level effectiveness to ensure that the new service was a success. The mistakes and misjudgements made at that time left a legacy which made the already difficult task of creating a successful new organisation even more difficult, and contributed significantly to some of the problems which are still being experienced. (Paragraph 32)

Tandem representation

5. The Minister for Children and the CAFCASS Board should make a definitive statement about their commitment to maintaining a system of tandem representation. These provisions are consistent with Article 12 of the United Nations Convention on the Rights of the Child. (Paragraph 52)

Review by the National Audit Office

6. We recommend that the National Audit Office review events [during CAFCASS's early days], including: use of the work of the Project Team; development of IT systems in CAFCASS; management of senior staff and use of consultants in the early months of CAFCASS; and events surrounding the departures of the Chief Executive and Director of Operations. (Paragraph 57)

Failures in service provision

7. In some places, there are no significant delays, and the service being provided by CAFCASS is as good as that which was provided by its predecessor service. In others, however—inner London, for example—delays have reached wholly unacceptable levels. (Paragraph 62)

Reasons for delay

8. The increase in demand—which did not start post-CAFCASS and should have been anticipated—and the shortage of appropriately qualified staff made it all the more important that CAFCASS hold on to the staff it was inheriting. The protracted dispute [with self-employed guardians] damaged relations with experienced guardians and staff the organisation desperately needed in order properly to fulfil one of its core functions. Key front-line practitioners were lost. (Paragraph 66)

Relations with other organisations

9. Full involvement by all concerned, CAFCASS staff included, in inter-agency initiatives and joint working is essential if disasters such as the Victoria Climbié affair are to be avoided in future. (Paragraph 92)

Research and improving practice

10. The ability of CAFCASS to evaluate the outcomes of its interventions—in other words, to identify 'what works' and to develop best practice accordingly—depends in part upon the development of a reliable data base that can be submitted to rigorous and detailed analysis. The development of a research-friendly culture, which welcomes external analysis and can work in partnership with the research community, will be central to the achievement of this goal. (Paragraph 96)

The "mixed economy"

11. It is important that, as well as using and developing its employed guardians, CAFCASS senior management embrace the principle of a mixed economy and repair relations with self-employed guardians. It would be unacceptable if some children and families were offered an inferior service because of the neglect of a significant part of the skilled available workforce. (Paragraph 111)

Relationship between LCD and CAFCASS

12. The Framework Document fails to reflect the proper relationship between the LCD and CAFCASS as established by the relevant legislation. The Framework Document also displays a curious, and worrying, lack of attention to CAFCASS's key role. (Paragraphs 114 and 117)

13. CAFCASS provides a vitally important service in which we would expect Ministers to take a close interest. The confusion over the terms on which they do so has resulted from the unclear constitutional relationship between LCD and CAFCASS. It has produced suspicions of inappropriate interference, has hampered efforts to establish a properly functioning service. (Paragraph 119)

The CAFCASS Board

14. It is clear that the confused lines of accountability between LCD, CAFCASS and the Senior Management Team, particularly the Chief Executive, are seriously hampering the Board's ability to make an effective contribution. The lack of relevant experience and expertise on the Board make it important that it is not reliant solely on the senior management team for information about the service. (Paragraph 123)

15. There is no doubt that [the Board] has failed to deal effectively with the task with which it is entrusted. The Board has not given the impression that it has any clear idea of how CAFCASS should be re-establishing itself as an effective organisation. (Paragraph 124)

Failures in service provision

16. We were pleased to hear the Chief Executive affirm CAFCASS's intention to aim for allocation of guardians within 48 hours. We hope that this target can be speedily achieved. It should be formally recognised in CAFCASS's performance targets. (Paragraph 130)

17. We recommend that CAFCASS set a separate target—which should be as close to 100% as it is reasonably possible to get—for the allocation of a guardian in time for the first hearing in [emergency] cases. (Paragraph 131)

18. CAFCASS should play a full part in improving the service given to children and families in the family courts, by improving its own performance and by contributing to joint efforts to reduce delay across the system. (Paragraph 132)

CAFCASS Legal

19. It is important that the shortage of staff in CAFCASS Legal is not forgotten as CAFCASS deals with the difficulties it is experiencing elsewhere in the service. We recommend that such resources be made available to CAFCASS Legal as to enable it at least to match the service provided before it by the Official Solicitor. (Paragraph 133)

Dealing with the backlog

20. [The measures which CAFCASS has taken to increase capacity and deal with the backlog] are all welcome, though there is little sign as yet that they have made a significant impact. We hope that the judicial case management protocol referred to above, to which CAFCASS has signed up, will decrease delay in care cases. The only way in which CAFCASS is truly going to get on top of its service delivery duties is by dealing with its staff shortage. (Paragraph 134)

Recruitment and workforce planning

21. We recommend that CAFCASS urgently undertake comprehensive workforce planning, in order to identify accurately current and future staffing requirements. (Paragraph 139)

Attracting back experienced guardians

22. We recommend that CAFCASS take further steps to target recruitment on experienced guardians. (Paragraph 140)

Longer-term recruitment

23. We recommend that CAFCASS follow up [the] suggestion [that it join the current drive to attract and to retain more talented people into the social work professions]. (Paragraph 141)

Induction training

24. It would be unacceptable for new recruits to continue to be allowed to undertake this important work without the benefit of a proper course of training. The task of ascertaining and communicating to the court the child's wishes and feelings, as part of the process of determining what is in the child's best interests, should be central to that training. (Paragraph 145)

Convergence

25. Convergence in the work of practitioners from the two different strands needs to be handled with respect for the different skills and knowledge people bring. Convergence cannot be carried forward in the absence of properly developed training and development programmes which give the necessary preparation and backup for those moving into new areas of work. (Paragraph 146)

Performance management

26. CAFCASS must also face the issue of performance management. In setting standards [for performance management] CAFCASS should seek to draw on the expertise of its existing workforce, and the bodies which represent them. It should involve the Board and organisations which represent parents or children and commission and

make use of research. Local managers will need training and support to carry out this function. (Paragraphs 147, 148 and 149)

Progress in the provision of training

27. CAFCASS must ensure that all four aspects of the training agenda—induction and substantive training for new recruits; induction training for experienced social workers who need introducing and orientating to CAFCASS; in-service training and professional development; and convergence training—are addressed by the establishment of a dedicated training and development strand within CAFCASS. We recommend that an individual Board member or sub-group with appropriate experience or expertise should oversee its development and ongoing work. (Paragraph 151)

Information Technology

28. There is an urgent need for an integrated case management system for CAFCASS. (Paragraph 152)

29. We recommend that CAFCASS re-establish a project board and give it the task of setting out a clear timetable for the establishment of a fully fledged case management system. An individual Board member or sub-group should oversee (not micro-manage) the project. The new Department may need to make additional resources available to secure this crucial aspect of CAFCASS's proper functioning to ensure the timely establishment of an appropriate system. (Paragraph 155)

Support services

30. Until the delivery of core services is secure, CAFCASS cannot risk diverting significant resources into developing support services. (Paragraph 156)

Need to indicate role in provision of support services

31. There is a feeling amongst voluntary organisations working in this field that CAFCASS's failure to give clear indication of the way it might look to develop this aspect of its remit is hindering the development of services by others. CAFCASS needs to make clear what long-term role it envisages for itself in the provision of support services for children and families experiencing relationship breakdown. (Paragraph 157)

32. We recommend that the Minister for Children consult with CAFCASS and other interested parties about a proposal that the organisation should take a strategic/co-ordinating/funding role for support services rather than providing them itself. (Paragraph 158)

Funding for support services

33. If CAFCASS is to make a significant long-term contribution to the development of support services, we expect the Department will need to increase funding further. (Paragraph 160)

Cooperation with other bodies

34. The development of CAFCASS's role in the provision of [support] services requires close consultation and cooperation with all other bodies, statutory and voluntary, working in this field. (Paragraph 161)

35. CAFCASS needs to work much more closely than appears to have been the case hitherto with the Legal Services Commission. We hope that close working will enable value for money to be achieved in the provision of appropriate services whilst avoiding the narrow self-interest apparent so far in relations between the two bodies. (Paragraphs 162 and 163)

36. CAFCASS must work together closely with others in the family justice and child protection system. The Minister for Children and the CAFCASS Board should urgently review the claim by the CAFCASS Managers Association that many front line managers are having to withdraw from liaison arrangements. CAFCASS should take steps to ensure that there is full co-operation at all times. (Paragraph 164)

37. The collection of children's services within the Department for Education and Skills provides an opportunity for CAFCASS to renew its links with other organisations working with children, and ensure that the joined-up working demanded by the Victoria Climbié case, and others before it, is achieved. (Paragraph 165)

Research and improving practice

38. There is, as MCSI has identified, a significant gap in knowledge about "what works" in family proceedings related work which CAFCASS needs to fill. It is vital for the sake of all the children with whom CAFCASS is concerned that it discovers what works for children experiencing family breakdown, establishes how its practitioners can best contribute to the well-being of children involved in court proceedings or their aftermath, and ensures that best practice is developed accordingly. The establishment of a practice development unit, which CAFCASS intends to have in place by December this year, is a step in the right direction. Significant further progress in the development of research capacity will, however, be needed if CAFCASS is to achieve those aims. (Paragraph 166)

Management and organisation culture

39. It is important that this Report is not seen merely as an endorsement of the criticisms which have been made about CAFCASS. It is vital that CAFCASS work together with the professional and voluntary organisations who have expressed their concerns to us to address the issues which have been raised in this Report, and it is equally vital that the organisations concerned recognise that, in the interests of the children they

serve, a positive climate now needs to be created. CAFCASS needs to be helped to use, develop and build on the considerable skills which exist among its personnel and to become the kind of quality organisation it was originally intended to be. (Paragraph 170)

40. If it is to regain the confidence of all those who work with and for it, CAFCASS needs to demonstrate clearly and unambiguously that it is putting children and young people first in all that it does. (Paragraph 171)

41. We recommend that the CAFCASS Board identify three or four key actions which it can take which will demonstrate that it is truly "putting children and young people first". Such a refocusing of priorities should work through into a longer-term position where CAFCASS judges all that it does against the question "Will this improve the service we offer to children and the courts?" (Paragraph 172)

42. We recommend that, rather than waiting to be shown how [a "light management touch"] might work, the CAFCASS Board establish a working group to discuss both with its own stakeholders and with others with relevant expertise outside the organisation how such an approach could be implemented. (Paragraph 173)

The Framework Document and CAFCASS's relationship with government

43. The transfer of responsibility for CAFCASS away from the Lord Chancellor's Department, as was, to the Department for Education and Skills offers an opportunity for a reassessment and recasting of the relationship between CAFCASS and its parent Department. (Paragraph 174)

44. We recommend that, when the Framework Document is redrafted to take account of the new Departmental responsibilities, the DfES ensure that the new document both explicitly reflects CAFCASS's core task of securing the welfare of children in court proceedings through representation and reporting, and sets out the proper constitutional relationship between CAFCASS as an NDPB and its parent Department. Whilst CAFCASS remains an NDPB its parent Department must ensure that it is able to function as such and must respect the independence from Government which comes with that status. (Paragraph 175)

The CAFCASS Board

45. It is a central recommendation of this Report that there should be a fundamental review of membership of the Board. We believe the Board needs people of experience and stature who can develop the strategy necessary to deliver an effective, child-centred service. (Paragraph 180)

46. The new Board must take steps to ensure that it is able to carry out effectively its function of providing strategic direction and holding senior management to account. (Paragraph 181)

Inspection regime

47. We recommend that joint inspection arrangements be established between the new Commission for Social Care Inspection (CSCI) and the CAFCASS Inspection Unit of HM Magistrates' Court Services Inspectorate (MCSI). (Paragraph 182)

Continued Parliamentary scrutiny of CAFCASS's work

48. We hope that there will continue to be active Parliamentary oversight of CAFCASS's important work, and of the progress being made in addressing the recommendations we make in this Report. The children CAFCASS serves deserve no less. (Paragraph 183)

Formal minutes

Tuesday 15 July 2003

Members present:

Mr A J Beith, in the Chair

Mr Peter Bottomley	Mr Hilton Dawson
Ross Cranston	Mr Clive Soley
Mrs Ann Cryer	Keith Vaz
Mr Jim Cunningham	Dr Alan Whitehead

The Committee deliberated.

Draft Report [Children and Family Court Advisory and Support Service (CAFCASS)], proposed by the Chairman, brought up and read.

Ordered, That the Chairman's draft Report be read a second time, paragraph by paragraph.

Paragraphs 1 to 183 read and agreed to.

Conclusions read and agreed to.

Summary read and agreed to.

Resolved, That the Report be the Third Report of the Committee to the House.

Ordered, That the Chairman do make the Report to the House.

Several papers were ordered to be appended to the Minutes of Evidence.

Ordered, That the Appendices to the Minutes of Evidence be reported to the House.

Ordered, That the provisions of Standing Order No 134 (Select Committees (Reports)) be applied to the Report.

[Adjourned till Wednesday 16 July at 5.00pm

Witnesses

Tuesday 8 April 2003 *Page*

Kit Chivers and **Arran Poyser**, HM Magistrates' Courts Service Inspectorate   Ev 1

Rt Hon Dame Elizabeth Butler-Sloss DBE and **Mr Justice Johnson,** High Court Family Division, **His Honour Judge Martin Allweis,** Northern Circuit and **District Judge Nicholas Crichton,** Inner London Family Proceedings Court   Ev 7

Tuesday 29 April 2003

Katherine Gieve, Solicitors' Family Law Association, **Peter Watson-Lee** and **Christina Blacklaws**, The Law Society   Ev 16

Judith Timms OBE, National Youth Advocacy Service, **Vicky Leach,** NCH and **Chris Osborne,** The Children's Society   Ev 22

Harry Fletcher, Fiona Roberts and **Liz Moxham**, NAPO (The Trade Union and Professional Association for Family Court and Probation Staff)   Ev 27

Tuesday 6 May 2003

Alison Paddle, Susan Bindman, Carol Edwards and **Michael Griffith-Jones,** NAGALRO   Ev 31

Liz Goldthorpe and **Richard White**, Association of Lawyers for Children, **Pat Monro** and **Hilary Lloyd**, The Law Society   Ev 37

Colin Barnes and **Julie Doughty**, CAFCASS Managers Association   Ev 42

Thursday 22 May 2003

Anthony Hewson and **Jonathan Tross**, Children and Family Court Advisory and Support Service (CAFCASS)   Ev 49

Rosie Winterton MP, Parliamentary Secretary, and **Sally Field**, Lord Chancellor's Department   Ev 59

List of written evidence

1	Mills & Reeve Solicitors (submitted by Stephen King)	Ev 67
2	Paul Robert Morris	Ev 69
3	Families Need Fathers	Ev 77
4	Jill Fitz Gibbon, Sussex Family Services Manager, Sussex Magistrates' Courts Committee	Ev 80
5	Women's Aid Federation of England	Ev 81
6	Tina Shaw (Employed Children's Guardian)	Ev 83
7	Judge David Tyzack QC (Sitting in Devon and Cornwall)	Ev 83
8	Ms K Butcher (Self-Employed Children's Guardian)	Ev 84
9	His Honour Judge Bryant (Designated Family Judge, Teesside Combined Court Centre)	Ev 85
10	Parentline Plus and National Council for One Parent Families	Ev 87
11	Cox, McQueen, Howard, Tain Solicitors	Ev 89
12	His Honour Judge Tony Mitchell (Designated Family Judge, Northampton)	Ev 91
13	Mary Wilder (Children's Guardian)	Ev 91
14	British Association for Adoption and Fostering (BAAF)	Ev 92
15	District Judge Nicholas Crichton (Inner London Family Proceedings Court)	Ev 94
16	The Magistrates' Association	Ev 96
17	His Honour Judge Hugh Jones (Pontypridd County Court)	Ev 98
18	The Association for Shared Parenting	Ev 99
19	Rose S Dagoo (Self-Employed Children's Guardian)	Ev 101
20	Mrs Margaret Huber (Family Court Advisor)	Ev 101
21	His Honour Judge Tom Corrie (Designated Family Judge, Oxford)	Ev 103
22	Inner London and City Family Panel	Ev 103
23	Self-Employed Guardians serving Family Courts on Teesside	Ev 104
24	Children and Family Court Advisory and Support Service (CAFCASS)	Ev 105
25	Peter Harris (Official Solicitor to the Supreme Court until August 1999)	Ev 111
26	Benedict Gray (Children's Guardian and Social Work Consultant)	Ev 117
27	Mrs Kathleen Webb (Solicitors Member of the Law Society Children Panel)	Ev 121
28	The Children's Society	Ev 122
29	Joan Hunt (Senior Research Fellow, Centre for Family Law and Policy, University of Oxford)	Ev 124
30	Veronica J Swenson (Children's Guardian)	Ev 128
31	Oliver Cyriax (Former Solicitor)	Ev 132
32	Mrs Ann Head (Children's Guardian)	Ev 135
33	Children Law UK	Ev 136
34	CAFCASS Managers Association	Ev 137
35	Judith Timms OBE, former Chief Executive, The National Youth Advocacy Service (NYAS)	Ev 139
36	Equal Parenting Council and The Coalition for Equal Parenting	Ev 147
37	British Association of Social Workers	Ev 151

38	The Hon Mr Justice Bodey (Family Division Liaison Judge for the North East Circuit)	Ev 152
39	Sue Justice (Self-Employed Children's Guardian)	Ev 152
40	NAPO (The Trade Union and Professional Association for Family Court and Probation Staff	Ev 153
41	Alan W Kelsall (former member of the Guardian ad Litem and Reporting Officers Panel (GALRO) Committee)	Ev 158
42	Self-Employed Guardians in the South West of England	Ev 159
43	NAGALRO (The Professional Association of Family Court Advisers and Independent Social Work Practitioners and Consultants)	Ev 160
44	Justices' Clerks' Society	Ev 171
45	Raymond Adrian Porter (Head of the Family Unit, Archers, Solicitors)	Ev 171
46	Solicitors Family Law Association (SFLA)	Ev 176
47	Family Law Bar Association	Ev 179
48	Jim Richards (Director, Catholic Children's Society (Westminster))	Ev 181
49	National Society for the Prevention of Cruelty to Children (NSPCC)	Ev 183
50	The Law Society	Ev 187
51	Dr A K Darwish (Consultant Child Psychiatrist, Brynffynnon Child and Family Service)	Ev 189
52	Association of Lawyers for Children	Ev 190
53	ManKind (*Only the Executive Summary of this submission has been printed. A copy of the full memorandum has been placed in the House of Commons Library, where it may be inspected by Members. Copies are also available to the public for inspection from the Record Office, House of Lords*)	Ev 200
54	Lord Chancellor's Department	Ev 202
55	President of Family Division, High Court Family Division Judges, Council of Circuit Judges, the Association of District Judges and the District Judges of the Principal Registry of the Family Division	Ev 206
56	NCH	Ev 209
57	Family Rights Group	Ev 212
58	Joe Kuipers	Ev 214
59	Barry Meteyard (Family Court Reporter)	Ev 217
60	Association of Directors of Social Services	Ev 218
61	HM Magistrates' Courts Service Inspectorate (MCSI)	Ev 220
62	Legal Services Commission	Ev 221
63	Judy Weleminsky (Member of the CAFCASS Board)	Ev 226
64	Rosie Winterton MP, Parliamentary Secretary, Lord Chancellor's Department	Ev 230
65	Children and Family Court Advisory and Support Service (CAFCASS)	Ev 234
66	CAFCASS Managers Association	Ev 238
67	Judith Timms OBE, former Chief Executive, The National Youth Advocacy Service (NYAS)	Ev 241
68	NAGALRO (The Professional Association of Family Court Advisers and Independent Social Work Practitioners and Consultants)	Ev 244
69	Association of Lawyers for Children	Ev 246
70	NCH	Ev 252

71   Mr Shaun Paul O'Connell on behalf of Fathers4Justice [Not printed] (*A copy of this memorandum has been placed in the House of Commons Library, where it may be inspected by Members. Copies are also available to the public for inspection from the Record Office, House of Lords*)

Reports from the Committee on the Lord Chancellor's Department

Session 2002–2003

First Report	Courts Bill	HC 526
Second Report	Judicial Appointments: lessons from the Scottish experience	HC 902

ISBN 0-215-01216-X